Highlights of the Story of Christianity

ALICE PARMELEE

You shall receive power when the Holy Spirit has come upon you; and you shall be my witnesses in Jerusalem and in all Judea and Samaria and to the end of the earth.

Acts 1.8

MOREHOUSE-BARLOW CO.
Wilton, Connecticut

The cover illustration depicts the scene in the upper room in Jerusalem described in the first chapter of *Acts* after the risen Christ had presented himself just earlier to the Apostles on the day of Pentecost. The followers of Jesus flank the kneeling figure of Mary in the center. This bas-relief panel is part of the large Ter Sanctus Reredos, which is set behind the High Altar in the National Cathedral in Washington, D.C. The *Reredos* was executed by Angelo Lualdi at the Lualdi Studio in Italy, 1935-36, and this particular panel is directly below the *Reredos'* centerpiece, the *Majestus* figure of Christ. Used by permission of the Cathedral Church of Saints Peter and Paul, Washington, D.C.

The Scripture quotations in this book, unless attributed otherwise, are from the Revised Standard Version of the Bible, copyrighted 1946, 1952, ©1971, 1973 by the Division of Christian Education of the National Council of the Churches of Christ in the U.S.A., and used by permission.

Copyright ©1980 Alice Parmelee
All rights reserved

Morehouse-Barlow Co., Inc.
78 Danbury Road, Wilton, Connecticut 06897

ISBN-0-8192-1274-1

Library of Congress Catalog Card Number 80-81098

Printed in the United States of America

Contents

Preface v

Part One **The Apostolic Age, A.D. 30-100**
Chapter 1 The Dawn of Christianity 1
Chapter 2 A Distinctive Faith Arises 9
Chapter 3 The Writing of the New Testament 13
Chapter 4 Jewish Christianity 15

Part Two **Defining and Defending the Faith, A.D. 100-300**
Chapter 5 The World into which Christianity Came ... 17
Chapter 6 Early Encounters with Heresy 20
Chapter 7 The Christian Bible Appears 23
Chapter 8 The Church Survives Persecution 26
Chapter 9 The Fathers of the Church 30

Part Three **The Triumph of the Church, A.D. 300-500**
Chapter 10 Christianity Becomes the Religion
           of the Roman Empire 37
Chapter 11 The Creed and the Scriptures 44
Chapter 12 New Churches and Enriched Worship 50
Chapter 13 Prominent Preachers and Leaders 55
Chapter 14 The Beginnings of Monasticism 60
Chapter 15 The Expansion of the Church 62

Part Four **The Middle Ages, A.D. 500-1500**
Chapter 16 The Church Survives the Breakdown
           of the Empire 65
Chapter 17 Monasticism 68
Chapter 18 Christian Learning—Scholasticism 75
Chapter 19 The Papacy 78
Chapter 20 The Crusades 85
Chapter 21 The Bible 89

Part Five **The Eastern Orthodox Churches, 1054-1980**
   Chapter 22 East and West in Conflict 96
   Chapter 23 The Eastern Empire and the Church 98
   Chapter 24 Gains and Losses in the East 99
   Chapter 25 Eastern Orthodoxy Today 103

Part Six **The Reformation, 1500-1600**
   Chapter 26 The Winds of Change 105
   Chapter 27 Desiderius Erasmus 109
   Chapter 28 Martin Luther 115
   Chapter 29 John Calvin 119
   Chapter 30 The English Church and Henry VIII 122
   Chapter 31 The Reigns of Edward VI and Mary 130
   Chapter 32 The Elizabethan Settlement 133
   Chapter 33 The Catholic Revival 139

Part Seven **Modern Christendom**
   Chapter 34 Aftermath of the Reformation 142
   Chapter 35 Christianity Comes to America 144
   Chapter 36 The Christian Community Today 152

Selected Bibliography 155

Index 156

Preface

This book is an attempt to review the long story of Christianity and to open a wide perspective on the past. Readers may thus gain a deeper understanding of the Christian community of today and perhaps a clue to its future. Like hundreds of books that have been, and will be, written about the history of the church, this one is, in a sense, a sequel to the first, contemporary report—the Acts of the Apostles.

Acts, of course, ends with Paul still alive and preaching the gospel in Rome. What happened next? How was the good news of Christ spread abroad after death had silenced the voices of all who had known him, including all the apostles and their immediate disciples? What accounts for the fact that the young Christian community, divided by differences and often persecuted, managed not only to survive the upheavals of the next two centuries but also to flourish and to prevail? Why did the church, the only voluntary, all-embracing association in the world, outlast empires, kingdoms, and a variety of social institutions? During the Middle Ages, the Reformation, and succeeding centuries, what powerful currents of life and thought shaped the world-wide Christian community in which we worship today?

In reporting events and tracing the ebb and flow of historical forces, I have tried to focus continually on the men and women of faith who kept Christianity true to its message and mission. Their inner vision, their prayers and deeds, and often their heroism all comprise the substance of Christianity's history. Though most of these people are nameless, some are listed in the Calendar of the Church

Year in the *Book of Common Prayer,* and certain of them are discussed in this book.

The Scriptures are the title-deeds of Christianity. They establish its truth, enhance its unity, and ever contribute to its resilience and renewal. To celebrate this fact, I have touched upon the writing of the New Testament as well as the formation of the canon. I have also traced the preservation of the Bible and its changing roles and interpretation throughout the nearly two thousand years that Christians have been a Bible-reading people.

For this rich and varied story, I have used the work of many authorities, too numerous to name, from the writer of the Book of Acts to today's scholars. In selecting from and simplifying an extensive body of knowledge, I have tried to avoid distorting the record. Though many people have assisted me in this undertaking, I would especially like to thank: Daniel Sullivan for his careful editing; and Powel Mills Dawley, Professor Emeritus of Church History of the General Theological Seminary, New York, for reading the manuscript and making valuable suggestions.

Alice Parmelee

Part One
The Apostolic Age
A.D. 30-100

Chapter 1 The Dawn of Christianity

When darkness settled over Jerusalem on Friday evening after the crucifixion, the mission of Jesus appeared to have ended in utter failure. The authorities counted upon his execution as a common criminal to discredit his movement and end it once and for all. While his body lay in a borrowed tomb throughout the Sabbath day, his disciples remained numb with shock and despair, mourning him whom they had hoped "was the one to redeem Israel" (Luke 24.21). There was also fear among his friends and followers as they remembered the mood of the mob that had shouted, "Crucify him!" For many days thereafter they would continue to meet behind closed doors.

Nothing seemed likely to endure of the meteoric ministry of Jesus in which he had healed many and inspired hundreds with a living hope. Not a sentence of the New Testament had been written, except possibly for a few sayings of Jesus hastily scribbled down by someone to aid an unsure memory. On Friday night and the succeeding Sabbath most of the rulers in Israel were satisfied that an obscure but troublesome Galilean prophet had been silenced. Even his friends had to acknowledge the collapse of all their hopes. But, as before in Israel's experience, victory was to emerge from defeat, for the "Good News" proclaimed by Jesus Christ would in less than three hundred years become the spiritual mainspring of the Roman Empire and eventually of western civilization.

How did it happen? Answers may be found in the Gospels and in the Book of Acts, which is the only contemporary history of the apostolic age. According to all four Gospels, Christian faith dawned on the first day of the week, the day that ever after Christians regarded as holy. On that day the women followers of Jesus brought spices and ointments to his tomb in order to prepare his body for burial.

The events that ensued are a mystery beyond logical explanation, yet they convinced the followers of Jesus that his death was not the end but the beginning. At first the disciples failed to understand the significance of the news brought to them by the women and characterized their report of an empty tomb and an angel's message as merely an "idle tale." Nevertheless, Peter and John ran out to the rock-hewn tomb to see for themselves and found it in fact empty.

Accounts differ as to which member of the apostolic company first believed that their Lord had indeed risen from the dead. It may have been the Beloved Disciple (John 20.8), or Mary Magdalene (John 20.11-18), or Peter (1 Corinthians 15.5). Soon all the disciples, even "doubting" Thomas, shared the resurrection faith, having themselves seen the risen Lord. Armed with this certainty, they were unmoved by the rumor circulated by the Jerusalem authorities who vainly attempted to explain the embarrassing fact of the empty tomb. The rumor that the disciples had stolen the body was soon recognized as false, for it was obvious that men and women who had planned and carried out a deception were incapable of being deceived by it themselves.

For the disciples the resurrection seemed to remove a blindfold from their eyes, and they began to comprehend the events of which they had been a part. The reality of the

The Dawn of Christianity

Metropolitan Museum of Art, gift of George Blumenthal

The Three Women at the Sepulcher—German (c. 1175)

According to three Gospel accounts (Matthew 28.1-8; Mark 16.1-8; Luke 24.1-11), the first news of the resurrection came from the women who found the tomb of Jesus empty. This walrus ivory plaque, which was probably part of an altar frontal, tells the story with faithfulness and sensitivity.

resurrection became the climax of Peter's proclamation at Pentecost, "The Jesus we speak of has been raised by God, as we can all bear witness" (Acts 2.32, NEB). The conviction did not fade but grew, for later Paul confidently wrote, "If Christ has not been raised, then our preaching is in vain and your faith is in vain" (1 Corinthians 15.14). The belief that Christ had risen marks the historical beginning of Christianity. It was not, as Charles H. Dodd asserts, "a belief that grew up within the church; it is the belief around which the church itself grew up."

The New Testament indicates that while the risen Christ remained with his little band of followers he taught them the deeper aspects of their faith and sketched for them the shape of Christianity's future development. Christianity, it has been said, was "born with a Bible in its cradle." During his ministry Jesus had often based his teachings on the ancient oracles of God, quoting from them and offering his own interpretations. According to Luke, the risen Christ reinterpreted the Bible for his disciples in the light of his resurrection, and he "opened their minds to understand the scriptures" (Luke 24.45). His interpretations ranged widely, for "he began with Moses and all the prophets, and explained to them the passages which referred to himself in every part of the scriptures" (Luke 24.27, NEB).

The ancient books handed down by their forefathers acquired new meaning when the disciples read in them foreshadowings of Christ's life, death, and resurrection, and they perceived that the Scriptural promises were fulfilled in him. As he himself had clearly stated of the Scriptures, "I have come not to abolish them but to fulfill them" (Matthew 5.17). The disciples understood that Christ's resurrection was the sign that God's long-awaited new reign on earth had already begun. The Jesus they had accompanied in Galilee and Judea they now knew as Lord and Christ. His fundamental reinterpretation of the Scriptures would become the basis of the apostolic preaching and the letters of Paul. It would also be the theme of the Gospels.

A chorus of living voices proclaiming all that Jesus had done added themselves to the testimony of the ancient Scriptures. These were the voices of his followers to whom Christ had declared, "You shall be my witnesses" (Acts 1.8). Witnesses they indeed became of all that "we have seen with our eyes, which we have looked upon and touched with our hands, concerning the word of life" (1 John 1.1).

To fill the twelfth apostolic place left vacant by the defection of Judas the disciples chose Matthias. In their eyes he was qualified to be an apostle because he had witnessed Christ's resurrection and had "accompanied us during all the time that the Lord Jesus went in and out among us, beginning from the baptism of John until the day when he was taken up from us" (Acts 1.21-22). In short, he could witness from personal knowledge. Even after the four Gospels had been written, people preferred the evidence of actual eyewitnesses of Jesus or their close followers to anything written in a book. As late as the middle of the 2nd century, Papias, bishop of Hieropolis, remembering his youth when followers of the original disciples were still alive, wrote:

> If anyone came my way who had been a follower of the Elders, I would enquire about the sayings of the Elders—what Andrew said, or Peter, or Philip, or Thomas, or James, or John, or Matthew, or any other of the Lord's disciples. . . . For I did not think I got so much profit from the contents of books as from the words of a living, abiding voice.

Not many days after the resurrection the waiting band of his followers received from the risen Christ his final command, "Go therefore and make disciples of all nations" (Matthew 28.19). To a group of Jews this was an unusual mandate, for Judaism had never been a missionary religion but the valued possession of a special people, the exclusive faith of Abraham's descendants.

An assurance of divine aid accompanied Christ's command, "Lo, I am with you always, to the close of the age." Finally, he promised, "You shall receive power when the Holy Spirit has come upon you" (Acts 1.8).

This promise was fulfilled on the day of Pentecost in an upper room in Jerusalem when the followers of Jesus experienced the coming of the Holy Spirit. They heard the rush of a mighty wind, saw flames as of fire, and spoke in other tongues. This gift of tongues signified to them that the message of Christ was to be proclaimed to all peoples. To the assembled brethren Pentecost was the day of the Lord foretold in the Scriptures. Its wonders manifested the power and exaltation of their risen Master whom they would henceforth worship as ever-living Lord.

Their experience of the Holy Spirit was a vivid awakening of the divine Spirit within them, the Spirit for which they had not yet formulated a theological explanation but knew as the gift promised by Christ (John 14.26; Acts 2.38-39). In the days to come this indwelling Spirit would be at work within these men and women, enabling them to "do beyond their doing, love beyond their loving, and pray beyond their praying."

Empowered by the Holy Spirit, Peter first addressed "the house of Israel," interpreting the events of Pentecost in terms of the prophecy of Joel and affirming the reality of the resurrection. Peter climaxed his speech by declaring, "therefore know assuredly that God has made him both Lord and Christ, this Jesus whom you crucified" (Acts 2.36).

"Cut to the heart" by Peter's words, the people asked, "What shall we do?" Excitement ran high: "signs and wonders" ensued; crowds of people were baptized in the name of Jesus Christ; and many, even of the priests, accepted

Jesus as the Messiah. At this early period the movement was indeed a vital rebirth of Judaism that expressed itself in a deepening devotion to God, in trust, in gratitude, and in awe. People began to see in the mission of Christ, in his life and death and resurrection, that God had opened a new avenue of approach to himself.

Believers in the living Lord remained faithful to the ancient Jewish Law and continued to worship in the Temple at the appointed hours of prayer, for they were convinced that theirs was not a new faith but the complete realization of the old. The Sadducees, however, became alarmed at the enthusiastic reception of the new message and forbade the apostles to preach in the name of Christ. Twice Peter and John were imprisoned. They were beaten. They were brought before the Sanhedrin. There the liberal rabbi Gamaliel defended them, warning his colleagues in words that proved to be prophetic, "If this plan or this undertaking is of men, it will fail; but if it is of God, you will not be able to overthrow them. You might even be found opposing God!" (Acts 5.39)

Despite official opposition, the vigorous new movement continued to expand. Its adherents "devoted themselves to the apostles' teaching and fellowship, to the breaking of bread and the prayers. . . . And all who believed were together and had all things in common; and they sold their possessions and goods and distributed them to all, as any had need" (Acts 2.42, 44-45). The apostles, as the accepted leaders, developed such strong bonds of fellowship within the movement that the needy were supported and "those who believed were of one heart and soul" (Acts 4.32). In this atmosphere of unity the apostles taught that Christ is the fulfillment of the Scriptures. They shared their memories of all that he had said and done, shaping and condensing through repetition the sayings and stories into those vivid literary units upon which the written Gospels were to be based.

In addition to teaching and fellowship there was daily worship not only with fellow Jews in the Temple but at special services in private homes belonging to the faithful. There "the breaking of bread" became a communal meal commemorating the last supper. At these gatherings portions of the Old Testament were read and interpreted in accordance with a synagogue custom which Jesus himself had practiced. Now, however, the interpretations were made in the light of Christ's teachings and resurrection.

Chapter 2 **A Distinctive Faith Arises**

Many Jews flocked to the new movement, instinctively drawn to its spiritual creativeness and human comradeship. They were impressed by the good news taught by the apostles and convinced that in Christ, God's revelation to Israel had reached its culmination. But some of the Jews could not accept Jesus as Messiah and Lord because they feared that this new teaching would destroy rather than fulfill their ancient faith. Their fear soon centered upon Stephen, a Greek-speaking Jewish Christian, or, in Biblical terms, a "Hellenist."

Stephen had been chosen by the apostles to help minister to his fellow Hellenists. At this time he perceived perhaps more clearly than did the original, Aramaic-speaking, Jewish Christians of Jerusalem that the teachings of Jesus, both implicitly and explicitly, were addressed to all peoples. The command to "make all nations my disciples" (Matthew 28.19, NEB) threatened the exclusive aspect of their Jewish faith.

When some of the Jews tried to argue with Stephen, they failed to prevail against the wisdom and eloquence with which he spoke of Christ. Angered, they seized him and brought him before the Sanhedrin. Stephen defended himself with a brilliant interpretation of history, but when he spoke of beholding the glorified Jesus "standing at the right hand of God" (Acts 7.56), those at the trial rioted. The Jews, believing his words to be blasphemy, dragged Stephen outside the city walls and stoned him to death.

Young Saul, at this time a fanatical defender of Judaism, watched this mob-murder with satisfaction. Yet Stephen's

Christ-like prayer of forgiveness for his murderers must have haunted Saul. It is possible that, as Augustine later remarked, "If Stephen had not prayed, the Church would not have had Paul." Later, on the Damascus road, Saul was himself converted to Christ and, taking the name of Paul, he resumed Stephen's work of extending the boundaries of Christianity.

This first Christian martyrdom demonstrated the truth of a well-known saying of the early 3rd-century theologian Tertullian that, "The blood of the martyrs is the seed of the church." After Stephen's death and the persecution that ensued, many Greek-speaking Christians fled from Jerusalem and began to preach the gospel of Christ throughout Judea, Samaria, Phoenicia, Cyprus, and Antioch. Though they appealed at first to Jews, their message reached Gentiles also.

According to Acts, Peter's conversion of the first Gentile, the centurion Cornelius, provoked sharp criticism from his fellow believers in Jerusalem (Acts 10.1-11.18). At this early period the church was faced with an issue that was to divide it deeply. Should Jewish Christians associate with Gentiles and eat with them, thus breaking the Law? Could a Gentile become a Christian without first fully complying with Jewish Law?

For the next decade or so after Stephen's death the apostles remained in comparative peace in the mother church in Jerusalem, the city of the Old Covenant, which had become even more holy to them because here Christ had established the New Covenant, here he had died and risen, and here the Holy Spirit had been given to the community of Christ's followers. During the persecutions of Herod the Great's grandson Herod Agrippa I, A.D. 42-44, James the apostle was beheaded and Peter arrested and imprisoned.

After this outbreak of violence the original apostles apparently scattered, and Acts ceases to trace their move-

A Distinctive Faith Arises

ments. Traditions and legends surround their subsequent lives. Both the church of Antioch and that of Rome claim Peter as founder. John is associated with Ephesus and Thomas with India where the Mar Thoma church continues to revere his memory.

In Jerusalem the leadership of the church passed to James, the Lord's brother (Mark 3.6). In A.D. 49 he presided over the council at which he proposed a compromise between the Jewish Christians and the small but rapidly expanding group of Gentiles (Acts 15.1-29). This compromise freed Gentiles from the ceremonial requirements of the Jewish Law, requirements that had prevented many Gentiles from accepting Christ. The final result of the compromise, however, was the gradual end of the Jewish dominance in the Christian community.

Many men and women, both named and unnamed in the New Testament, brought the message of Christ to the Gentiles. Paul, of course, is the best known of them all. During his far-flung missionary journeys he was always at the advancing edge of the Christian movement, whether in Antioch, where the disciples were first called "Christians," Cyprus, Asia Minor, Greece, or Rome. Wherever he went, the Jews and even the Jewish Christians attacked him as a renegade from his native faith. But Paul's background of Pharisaism, his rabbinic training, his familiarity with Greek thought, his understanding of the apostolic teaching, and, above all, his intense personal devotion to Christ, all helped him withstand opposition and gave him a deeper insight into the teaching and significance of Christ than perhaps any other of the early Christian leaders.

Paul was convinced that to the people of Israel "belong the sonship, the glory, the covenants, the giving of the law, the worship, and the promises; to them belong the patriarchs, and of their race, according to the flesh, is the Christ" (Romans 9.4-5). It was to his "brethren, my kinsmen by race," that Paul and the other early missionaries first carried the good news of Christ. They visited the network of synagogues throughout the Jewish Diaspora, trying to convince the Jews that God's revelation to Israel had finally culminated in Christ. Whenever Paul's words failed to convince the Jews and they turned against him and reviled him, as occurred in Antioch of Pisidia, he appealed to the Gentiles (Acts 13.46-47). Thus Paul's mission became more and more a mission to the Gentiles. Though he founded many Gentile churches around the shores of the Mediterranean, he always made an attempt to bridge the differences between his converts and the Jewish Christians of Jerusalem. Once he wrote "in great grief and unceasing sorrow" concerning his failure to win his own people to faith in Christ, their Messiah. In agony of spirit he declared, "For I could even pray to be outcast from Christ myself for the sake of my brothers, my natural kinsfolk" (Romans 9.3, NEB). He himself remained a loyal Jew and his last recorded act as a free man was to fulfill his ritual obligations under the Jewish Law (Acts 21.15-26).

The gospel of Christ preached by Paul, however, transcended Judaism and its Law. "It is no longer I who live, but Christ who lives in me," he wrote. And he added:

> For as many of you as were baptized into Christ have put on Christ. There is neither Jew nor Greek, there is neither slave nor free, there is neither male nor female; for you are all one in Christ Jesus. And if you are Christ's, then you are Abraham's offspring, heirs according to promise.
>
> Galatians 2.20; 3.27-29

Chapter 3 The Writing of the New Testament

The story of the writing of the New Testament, a story far better understood today than in an earlier period, still remains full of uncertainties and disputed dates. One thing, however, is generally agreed upon by scholars: that Paul's First Letter to the Thessalonians, written from Corinth c. A.D. 50, is the oldest New Testament document that survives in its original form. With this letter and the great series of Paul's letters that followed, the writing of the New Testament began. Neither Paul nor the churches to whom he wrote regarded these communications as Scripture, yet such they eventually became when people recognized them to be authentic expressions of the Christian faith.

Paul's mission to the Gentiles ended about A.D. 64 when, according to tradition, he and Peter died in Rome among the Christian martyrs in Nero's persecution. After the apostolic voices fell silent the second generation of witnesses had to rely increasingly upon documentary sources for the facts upon which the good news of Christ was based. During this period Paul's letters were collected, copied, and circulated among the churches, so that by c. 150, when the last New Testament book was written, its author assumes that Paul's writings are veritable Scripture (2 Peter 3.15-16).

In addition to these letters the church collected stories and sayings of Jesus and incidents in his life. They also assembled Old Testament texts that related to his mission. Soon these materials must have been written down to provide Christian missionaries and teachers with reliable information. From documents like these and from the personal memories of people who had heard the apostles preach, the Gospel of Mark is believed to have been compiled sometime between the years 65 and 75. A short time later two other authors may have revised the Gospel of Mark, adding material from their own sources and adapting their presentation to their own particular audiences. Thus the Gospels of Matthew and Luke were quite likely produced. Probably near the end of the 1st century, a fourth evangelist, writing from an independent point of view and deriving little if anything from the earlier Gospels, published the Gospel of John.

All four of these Gospels as well as Acts were written, as might have been expected, not in the Aramaic tongue spoken by Jesus and his disciples but in Greek, the language spoken everywhere throughout the Roman Empire during the 1st and 2nd centuries. Undoubtedly the evangelists translated some of their sources from Aramaic, and indeed a few Aramaic words still remain in the Gospels, but few scholars today believe that the Gospels themselves were originally written in Aramaic. It seems more likely that the four Gospels and Acts were written, as were Paul's letters, for the Greek-speaking Gentile church in order to present Christ to the entire Greco-Roman world.

Chapter 4 **Jewish Christianity**

While Gentile Christianity was expanding and producing its basic documents, Jewish Christianity carried on the mission of Jesus to his own people, the people of Israel. For about twenty years James, the Lord's brother, presided over the mother church at Jerusalem, which remained one of the sects within Judaism. During an outburst of religious fanaticism preceding the Jewish war the Christian community sought refuge across the Jordan in the Gentile city of Pella. In this city of the Decapolis the Christians escaped the destruction of Jerusalem by the Romans in A.D. 70.

After the holocaust, when the Jewish Christians returned to the Holy City, they chose James's nephew Simeon as their head, for this office apparently had become hereditary in the family of Jesus. According to the 4th-century church historian Eusebius, "Those who were called brothers . . . governed the entire church in virtue of their being martyrs and relatives of the Lord."

Under a succession of fifteen bishops who remained practicing Jews, Jewish Christianity struggled on in Palestine until A.D. 135. As it gradually became depleted in numbers and wealth, it failed to attract leaders of outstanding intelligence, with the result that the once dominant Palestinian church was no longer comparable to the vigorous church of the Gentiles. When the Jews rebelled against their Roman overlords in 132 and claimed that their fanatical leader Simon Bar Kosiba was the messiah come to rescue Israel, the mother church of the apostolic age, being unable to accept this claim, lost its connection with Judaism and faded away. Thus, after the century during which Paul and others labored to convince the Jews that Christ was the fulfillment of God's promises to Israel, Judaism and Christianity became completely divided.

On the site of Jerusalem, destroyed at the end of Bar Kosiba's disastrous rebellion, the Romans built a colonial city named *Aelia Capitolina*. Its plan still underlies the Jerusalem of today. It contained a theater, circus, baths, colonnades, monumental gates, and statues of Jupiter and the Emperor Hadrian in the former Temple area. Though Jews and also Christians of Jewish origin were excluded from the city, Christians of foreign birth soon arrived to establish a new Christian community ruled by Gentile bishops.

Early in the 3rd century the Gentile Christians of *Aelia* began to welcome a stream of pilgrims who practiced a new form of piety. According to Melito, bishop of Sardis, they came to see "the place where the gospel was proclaimed and the gospel history was acted out." Here also Bishop Alexander Flavian established a library in 212 that was later to furnish invaluable materials on early church history to such scholars as Origen, Eusebius, and Jerome.

Part Two
Defining and Defending the Faith A.D. 100-300

Chapter 5 The World Into Which Christianity Came

Rome dominated the world of the young church. With military might and political astuteness the empire imposed an uneasy unity upon many different peoples, allowing them considerable scope in which to practice their own customs, languages, and religions. Roman law, however, was standard throughout the empire, so that Paul, as a Jew with Roman citizenship, was entitled to appeal his case from the provincial court in Caesarea to a higher imperial court in Rome. Protected sea lanes in the Mediterranean and excellent Roman roads linking all parts of the empire, though established primarily for the movement of armies and the exchange of commercial goods, facilitated the spread of Christianity.

By the time Christianity reached the main cities of the Mediterranean world, the old Roman gods had lost their appeal and the empire lacked a religious center. In order to satisfy their spiritual needs the Romans turned to a variety of faiths among which were the Greco-Oriental mystery religions. Such nature goddesses as the Great Mother Cybele of Asia Minor, and Isis, the Egyptian goddess of fertility and magic, attracted crowds of worshipers. Many Romans lived according to the high ethical standards and attended the sacramental rites of the cult of Mithras, the Persian deity of light and wisdom. This soldiers' cult became a serious rival to Christianity. Though less popular than these mystery religions, Judaism, as the New Testament indicates, made some proselytes among the Gentiles, primarily because it emphasized a holy God and moral conduct. But Judaism, despite the words of the prophets about universal salvation (Isaiah 45.22-23, etc.), was basically the religion of a special people and therefore it failed to appeal to great numbers of Romans.

Christianity combined the best of the current religions. It was both moral and mystical. It opposed the evils that destroy men and women, and it satisfied their need to find meaning in their lives. Christian faith centered in one holy God, the Father of all people, whose Son Jesus Christ is the guarantee of the Father's love. It taught that communion with God through Jesus Christ is possible for those who live in uprightness and faith. As Augustine, the great Church Father from North Africa, later observed, "It gave ordinary people the ability to live out a code of conduct formerly attained by only a few philosophers."

During the 2nd and 3rd centuries the triumph of Christianity remained a remote dream, so great were the problems and dangers facing the church. After freeing itself from political and religious bondage to Judaism in the 1st century, Christianity met competition from the mystery religions as well as persecution from the state. Even within its own community heresies arose from which it had to defend itself. It was faced with the tasks of defining its faith, outliving its competitors, and withstanding persecution. Also, it had to convert the barbarians poised to overrun the empire, while at the same time creating an organization capable of surviving the collapse of Roman civilization and the decline and fall of the empire. In responding to these challenges, the church attracted to itself and nurtured the most creative minds of the period and kept alive the skills and learning of Rome, Greece, and Egypt. Amid all the upheavals of the early Middle Ages, it established a new unity in Western Europe centered in the only voluntary, all-embracing association in the world. Finally, the church brought a new civilization to birth.

Chapter 6 Early Encounters with Heresy

The vitality of Christianity and its growing popularity attracted a host of pseudo-Christians. Acts contains a veritable rogues gallery of those who, even in the earliest years, tried to take advantage of the new faith: the deceiving couple, Ananias and Sapphira; Simon, from whose name comes the word "simony"; Elymas, the sorcerer of Cyprus; the soothsayers of Philippi; Sceva's sons, who acted as itinerant exorcists.

These easily identified false friends of Christianity were of less danger to the church, however, than the heretical sects that soon tried to modify the gospel according to their particular, and often strange, ideas. Because the Christian community welcomed everyone and offered freedom to all its members, it created an atmosphere in which new ideas and doctrines flourished. Some of these contributed to the life of the church and deepened its understanding of the gospel, but others, by their exclusiveness and rigidity, stirred up disputes that threatened to undermine the Christian faith. Five New Testament letters written between the years 80 and 150 (Hebrews, 1 and 2 Peter, James, and Jude) reflect these disputes. During these years the church, in its need for authentic teachings, turned to Paul's collected letters and the recently completed Gospels to learn from first- and secondhand witnesses "the truth concerning the things of which you have been informed" (Luke 1.4).

Needing convenient and easily read documents with which to refute heretics, instruct the faithful, and appeal to unbelievers, the church adopted the newly developed book form known as the codex. For its day it was comparable to the invention of radio or television in the 20th century. The codex was a papyrus or parchment book with pages like those of a modern book. It was less bulky than the scroll on which the Scriptures had traditionally been written, and it proved to be effective for its purpose. The church was apparently the chief pioneer in the use of this new mode of communication, because most of the codices surviving from the 2nd and 3rd centuries contain Christian literature.

Gnosticism faced Christianity with its most serious peril since Paul's struggle for freedom from the Jewish Law. An early form of Gnosticism is referred to in Paul's Letter to the Colossians and in the First Letter of John. Gnosticism was an esoteric movement combining Greek philosophy, various eastern religions, Jewish apocalyptic teachings, and elements of Christian thought, all merged in a body of secret "knowledge" that promised salvation to those capable of spiritual enlightenment. The Gnostics rejected God the Creator because they regarded matter as evil and despaired of gaining happiness in this world. Moreover, they denied that Christ had been truly a man who lived and suffered and died on the cross as a human being. They taught that he was really a spiritual symbol, a god appearing in the guise of a man. This dogma was completely opposed to the apostolic testimony that Christ had been "manifested in the flesh" (1 Timothy 3.16).

The threat that Gnosticism posed for Christianity was all the greater because some of the keenest minds and most devoted teachers in the church were at various times attracted to this popular movement and wrote extensively about it. Among the Gnostic documents that have survived are forty-six found at Nag-Hamadi in Upper Egypt in 1946. Three of these are entitled gospels: the *Gospel According to Thomas,* the *Gospel of Philip,* and the *Gospel of Truth.* All are written in Coptic and contain sayings of Jesus most of which were apparently derived from the canonical Gospels. Some of the sayings, however, were previously unknown and may be genuine additions to the legacy of Christianity.

An effective defender of the church against Gnosticism was Irenaeus, a deeply religious man born in Asia Minor. He was trained as a disciple of Polycarp in Smyrna, eventually became bishop of Lyons in southern Gaul, and is regarded as one of the early Fathers of the Church. His most important work, *Against Heresies*, written c. 185, effectively pointed out that Gnostic teaching was basically contrary to the historic Christian faith.

During the 2nd century the Christian communities gradually expelled the Gnostics. As a result of this experience with heretics, the church began to formulate its faith in statements expressed in the form of questions which candidates for baptism were required to endorse. The earliest creeds had simply stated, "Jesus is Lord" (1 Corinthians 12.3), but by the 3rd century the church in Rome asked of its candidates:

> Do you believe in God the Father Almighty? Do you believe in Jesus Christ the Son of God, who was born of the Holy Spirit and the Virgin Mary, who was crucified under Pontius Pilate and died, and rose the third day living from the dead, and ascended into heaven, and sat down at the right hand of the Father, and will come to judge the living and the dead? Do you believe in the Holy Spirit, and the Holy Church, and the resurrection of the flesh?

With additions made to guard against other heresies and with the baptismal questions turned into declarations, the present Apostles' Creed emerged.

Chapter 7 The Christian Bible Appears

From its earliest days the church venerated the Septuagint, which was the Old Testament in Greek, and regarded it as Holy Scripture. The apostles and teachers constantly referred to it and read portions of it during services of worship. Before long the early Christian writings, including Paul's letters (2 Peter 3.15-16) and the Gospels, began to be read in addition to the Septuagint. Justin Martyr, in his *Apology* written in Rome c. 150, describes the Sunday service there as commencing with a reading from the Gospels followed by the Old Testament:

> The memoirs of the apostles [Gospels] or the writings of the prophets are read as long as we have time. Then, when the reader has finished, the president speaks, admonishing and exhorting us to the imitation of these excellent things. After that we rise all together and offer prayer. And when the prayer has ended, bread and wine and water are presented.

Marcion, a wealthy shipowner from Pontus on the Black Sea, was the son of a Christian bishop. He went to Rome, c. 140, to gain support for his proposal to adopt a "New" Testament. After generously contributing a large amount of money to the charitable work of the church, he outlined his ideas. Having been influenced by Gnostic teachings, Marcion believed that the God of the Old Testament represented evil and that to restore Christ's gospel to its original purity it must be freed from its Jewish background. He proposed that the entire Septuagint be rejected and that a treatise written by himself, together with drastically censored editions of the Gospel of Luke and of Paul's letters, should become the "New" Testament. Though Marcion attracted a large following, the church in Rome rejected his Gnostic ideas as heretical, returned the money he had contributed, and excommunicated him.

Undeterred by this rebuff, Marcion founded a new Gnostic sect known as the Marcionites. This sect was powerful enough to survive into the 5th century. In denying Christ's humanity, Marcion and his followers set aside the evidence in the Gospels and a basic teaching of the church. In rejecting the Old Testament, they repudiated the church's faith in Christ as the fulfillment of the Scriptures and the culmination of God's revelation to Israel.

The church met the two-fold Gnostic attack by reaffirming the Scriptural basis of its faith, defining its beliefs, and discarding books that promoted strange doctrines. Its most practical counterattack consisted in listing those works which truly expressed its faith.

Many apocryphal gospels had been written by 170 when Tatian, a Syrian Christian, compiled a gospel for use in his evangelistic work northeast of Syria in the Kingdom of Edessa. By carefully fitting together a mosaic of quotations from Matthew, Mark, Luke, and John, Tatian produced a single, continuous narrative of Jesus' life. This was called the *Diatessaron,* meaning "the four Gospels in one", but nicknamed the "Scissors and Paste Gospel." Though compiled probably in Syriac, Tatian's work was soon translated into Greek. The fact that he rejected the apocryphal gospels and used only the four that were later declared canonical proves that before the beginning of the 3rd century the four Gospels had already attained their pre-eminence as authoritative writings. Fortunately, because Tatian's method of harmonizing the Gospels was not widely adopted, the uniqueness of each work was preserved, not lost, as had been the fate of the original documents plowed under by the compilers of the Old Testament books from Genesis to Deuteronomy and beyond.

A Latin manuscript now known as the Muratorian Fragment is thought to have originated in the church at Rome c. 200. It acknowledges as sacred Scripture all the present New Testament books except Hebrews, James, 1 and 2 Peter, and 3 John, the authenticity of which were being discussed. The Muratorian Fragment includes only two of the many works that were ultimately judged apocryphal: the Wisdom of Solomon and the Apocalypse of Peter. Of the latter book, however, the Fragment indicates the contemporary uncertainty, saying, "some of our own [bishops] will not allow it to be read in church."

Eventually, the spiritual quality and timeless value of the documents produced under the personal influence of the apostles and their early followers became evident, and these books were declared to be Scripture. The oldest-surviving list of the twenty-seven books of the New Testament canon appears in the Easter letter addressed to the clergy of his diocese in 367 by Athanasius, patriarch of Alexandria.

Chapter 8 The Church Survives Persecution

During the church's first century of quiet, steady growth it remained relatively obscure and powerless, suffering only local and sporadic persecution. As has already been noted, a Jewish mob murdered Stephen; Saul harassed the Lord's disciples; Herod Agrippa executed the apostle James and arrested Peter; and Paul was often set upon and imprisoned. Even Nero's massacre of many Roman Christians, including probably Peter and Paul, was not so much a matter of imperial policy as an attempt to blame Rome's disastrous fire on convenient scapegoats.

Toward the end of the century, however, the "Christian problem" began to worry Roman rulers. As the New Testament indicates (1 Peter 4.12-17; Revelation 2.10), the church braced itself for an official persecution ordered by the Emperor Domitian (81-96). One of its victims was the author of Revelation, who was evidently condemned to forced labor in the stone quarries on the island of Patmos lying offshore from Asia Minor (Revelation 1.9). Another victim was the emperor's cousin, the consul Flavius Clemens, who was sentenced to death in A.D. 95, possibly because of his Christian beliefs, and whose wife Flavia Domitilla was banished. One of the oldest catacombs of the church in Rome belonged to Domitilla.

Despite persecution, so many prominent and educated people had been converted to the new faith by the time of Trajan's reign (98-117) that Christianity was a force to be reckoned with. Rome's general policy of religious tolerance for all kinds of sects did not apply to Christians because they rejected the state religion and the old gods of Rome and firmly refused to burn incense to the emperor as a god. The authorities charged Christians with atheism, anarchy, and treason and declared their religion illegal. Anyone accused of believing in Christ was liable to decapitation, a punishment that could be avoided simply by denying Christ and worshiping the Roman gods. Though individual Christians were seldom sought out and brought to trial, they lived under continual threat of persecution. Many of them recanted when excited mobs screamed accusations, but some chose martyrdom as the ultimate witness to their faith in the Lord Jesus Christ.

One of the latter was Ignatius, bishop of Antioch. Journeying to Rome as a prisoner c. 110, he wrote of his approaching martyrdom in the amphitheater, "I bid all men know that of my own free will I die for God. . . . I am God's wheat and I am ground by the wild beasts that I may be found the pure bread of Christ." Ignatius may have been a personal disciple of John the Evangelist. He resisted Gnosticism, upheld church unity, and was the first to describe the church as "catholic," meaning "universal" as opposed to particular.

Another famous martyr was Polycarp, a friend of Ignatius and the bishop of Smyrna in Asia Minor. In 156, as an old man, Polycarp returned from a mission to Rome to find Smyrna in a frenzy of anti-Christian disorder, with the mob demanding, "Away with the atheists!" Then they shouted, "Let search be made for Polycarp!" The city officials advised the aged bishop to recant and "revile Christ," but Polycarp replied, "Eighty-six years have I served him and he has done me no wrong. How then can I speak evil of my King and my Savior?" The mob had its way and Polycarp died with dignity and courage in the flames of a pyre. He may have been the last survivor of those who had spoken with men and women who had known Jesus face to face.

Under Marcus Aurelius (161-180), an otherwise humane and learned emperor, the church suffered bitter and widespread persecution. This was largely because the emperor was convinced that Christianity caused the troubles besetting his reign. At this time the Church Father Justin, called the Martyr, was put to death in Rome with some of his disciples.

The empire declined visibly after Marcus Aurelius. Populations diminished, commerce dwindled, taxes increased. As the government became incompetent, boundary defenses were poorly maintained, and the many barbarians recruited into the army began to diminish its former strength. All these misfortunes were blamed on the growing number of Christians, who by their rejection of the gods were believed to have angered the deities on whom the well-being of Rome depended. Officially, therefore, Christianity remained illegal. Practically, however, the church suffered only intermittent persecution and, on the whole, enjoyed a century of considerable toleration during which it continued to increase in numbers and strength.

Decius (249-251) instituted the first systematic and general persecution of all Christians who refused to sacrifice to the emperor, a policy resolutely carried out with great brutality for a decade. During this period, Origen, the illustrious Biblical scholar and one of the greatest of the Greek theologians, died as a result of torture.

The final and most terrible persecution occurred under Diocletian (284-305). Determined to bring order out of the chaos into which the empire was falling, he issued four edicts against Christians. Their assemblies were forbidden, churches destroyed, Scriptures burned, and clergy tortured and put to death. Wealthy Christians were banished and their estates seized. All Christians were required to sacrifice to the gods and to the emperor as a god. Since earliest times Christians had obeyed the laws and, as 1 Timothy

The Church Survives Persecution 29

2.1-2 indicates, they customarily prayed *for* the emperor and all in authority, but they steadfastly refused to pray *to* him. When put to the test a few of them recanted, but during this persecution the list of the martyrs lengthened. The campaign of terror spread throughout the empire. There is a tradition that at this time Britain's first martyr, a former Roman soldier named Alban, was executed at Verulamium near London because he had sheltered a Christian priest. In the end, Diocletian's policy failed and the church emerged triumphant from its ordeal, inspired by the courage and steadfastness of its martyrs and strengthened by the vitality of its faith.

Chapter 9 The Fathers of the Church

While the church was combatting heresies, formulating its beliefs, establishing the canon of the New Testament, and withstanding persecution, it produced a group of saintly men whose writings constitute the literature of Christianity during the centuries following the apostolic age. These bishops, theologians, teachers, and scholars were keen of intellect, possessed of good judgment, and well versed in the Scriptures. They are called the Fathers of the Church and their teachings were considered authoritative in matters of faith and practice. Their writings provide invaluable information concerning Christian tradition and belief, church history, and the canonization of the Scriptures. The fact that their Scriptural quotations are from an early text of the New Testament makes their works significant to textual scholars. The collected writings of the Church Fathers from the apostolic age to the Middle Ages fill scores of volumes.

The earliest Fathers of the Church, because they may have known either the apostles or their immediate disciples, are often designated as the "Apostolic Fathers," though "sub-apostolic" would be more accurate. Some of the works of this early group are contemporary with the later New Testament books. The *Epistle of Barnabas,* the *Shepherd of Hermas,* and *1 Clement* and *2 Clement* were once included in the New Testament Scriptures. The first two, for instance, appear in the 4th-century Codex Sinaiticus and the last two in the 5th-century Codex Alexandrinus. Most of the Apostolic Fathers were not primarily literary men but wrote, like Paul, to meet an urgent need of the hour; consequently, they produced "human documents" that express their personal response to Christianity.

The works of the Apostolic Fathers include the following documents:

> The *Epistle of Barnabas*, by an unknown teacher writing between 78 and 120, describes the superiority of Christianity over Judaism and offers moral instruction.
>
> The *Two Epistles of Clement*. The first document, *1 Clement*, is attributed to an early bishop of Rome, a reputed disciple of Peter. It is an official communication, c. A.D. 96, from the church in Rome to the church in Corinth, and it mentions a threefold ministry. *2 Clement*, written between 120 and 160, is an anonymous sermon on ethical themes.
>
> The *Epistles of Ignatius* comprise seven letters written c. 110 by the bishop of Antioch on his journey to Rome and martyrdom.
>
> The *Epistle of Polycarp*, by the bishop of Smyrna to the church in Philippi, c. 115, asks about the fate of his friend Ignatius. The importance of the Scriptures in the early church is suggested by his words, "I trust you are well exercised in the Scriptures."
>
> The *Martyrdom of Polycarp*, written c. 155, gives an eyewitness account of Polycarp's death in Smyrna.
>
> The *Shepherd of Hermas* is an apocalypse containing moral teachings by the Roman Christian, Hermas, who may have been the brother of Pius, bishop of Rome c. 140.
>
> The *Didache*, or the *Teaching of the Twelve Apostles*, gives instructions concerning Christian teaching, worship, and the ministry, c. 90.

Fragments from Papias, by the bishop of Hieropolis, c. 145, contains his collection of the treasured sayings of those who had known Jesus. Papias is the author of two much-quoted statements: "Mark, having become the interpreter of Peter, wrote down accurately everything he remembered;" and Matthew "put in order" the oracles [sayings] of the Lord in Aramaic, which "each one interpreted as he was able."

The *Epistle to Diognetus*, an anonymous work of unknown date, describes Christians as "the soul of the world." It declares that they "are not different from other men. . . . They follow local customs of eating and living. They marry like everyone else, they have children, but they do not practice infanticide. . . . They spend their existence upon earth, but their citizenship is in heaven. They obey the established laws, and in their own lives they surpass the laws."

During the 2nd and 3rd centuries, while some of the Fathers of the Church were defending the faith against heresy, others presented the intellectual aspects of Christianity to educated pagans. So successful was this effort that the church won its struggle against paganism, giving succeeding Christian writers in the golden age of patristic literature an opportunity to deal with theological questions and interpret the Scriptures.

Accounts of six of the best-known Fathers of the Church during the 2nd and 3rd centuries follow:

Justin Martyr (c. 100-165), born at Shechem in ancient Samaria, became a Greek philosopher. While studying Plato, he was attracted to the Hebrew prophets and "the men who are the friends of Christ." He became convinced that their explanation "of the beginning and end of things" was true. His central belief was that Christianity is the oldest, truest, and most divine of the philosophies. When he traveled from place to place to teach, he wore his distinctive philosopher's cloak as a sign of his professional standing. In Rome he established a school in which he lectured on faith and morals and explained the Scriptures. One of his pupils was Tatian, who later compiled the Diatessaron. Justin, in his *Apology* and *Dialogue with Trypho*, defended Christianity against heathen criticism, Jewish objections, and the accusations of the state. His martyrdom in Rome, as was mentioned above, won him the name "Martyr."

Irenaeus (c. 120-200), the first great theologian, was the earliest Church Father to arrange Christian teachings in a comprehensive order. In his chief work, *Against Heresies*, he stated that Christ is "the only true and steadfast Teacher, the Word of God, our Lord Jesus Christ, who did through his transcendent love become what we are, that he might bring us to be even what he is himself." He was among the first to declare that the Christian writings based on apostolic teachings were as authoritative as the Old Testament Scriptures.

Clement of Alexandria (c. 150-215) became the second headmaster of the catechetical school in Alexandria. This famous institution was virtually a Christian university attended by converts as well as advanced students of the Scriptures. Clement recommended that new Christians read the Bible at home before the chief meal of the day. He also suggested that married couples read it together. Clement was the first to combine Platonism with Christianity. Obviously referring to Galatians 3.23-24, he wrote ". . . philosophy was given to the Greeks, till the Lord should call the Greeks. For this was a schoolmaster to bring the Hellenic mind, as the law brought the Hebrews, to Christ."

Tertullian (c. 160-230), the most formidable defender of faith in his day, was born in Carthage in North Africa. He became a lawyer, was converted to Christianity in Rome c. 190, and was the first prominent Christian writer to use Latin. His *Apology*, written in a vigorous, readable style, indicates the range of his learning and illustrates his ability to explain Christianity clearly and precisely. He gave form and impressiveness to Christian concepts. Among his well-known sayings are: "Christians are not born so, but born again." "Faith fears not famine." "The blood of the martyrs is the seed of the Church." He records the outreach of Christianity, including its eastward advance into Mesopotamia, Persia, and the frontiers of India, but he was more familiar with the churches of North Africa, Spain, and Gaul. His statement that, "Places of the Britains, unreached by the Romans, are subject to the law of Christ," is the oldest surviving literary record that, as early as the year 200, there were Christian missionaries in Britain.

Cyprian (c. 220-258), an educated man of wealth, became bishop of Carthage and was one of the most powerful leaders of the church. After his conversion at a mature age he was known for his kindliness and good judgment. He helped the church formulate its policy toward "lapsed" Christians who, from understandable human weakness, had denied Christ rather than face martyrdom. He urged that the Church give these Christians a second chance. He himself avoided one persecution by fleeing. Yet when he was again put to the test eight years later, he remained steadfast in his faith and accepted martyrdom.

Origen (c. 182-251), the greatest of the early theologians, was born in Alexandria of Christian parents who taught him the Scriptures at an early age. When his father died a martyr, young Origen desired to join him in this ultimate witness to Christ, but his mother prevented him. At eighteen he became headmaster of the catechetical school at Alexandria where some of the most distinguished leaders of the

Eastern Church were educated. As a teacher he accepted no fees from his students, but copied manuscripts to earn the little he needed to support his ascetic life. Later, after moving to Caesarea in Palestine, he established there the renowned school attended by the historian Eusebius.

Origen excelled in many fields of scholarship. His book, *On First Principles*, written before 231, was, in Williston Walker's words, "not merely the first great systematic presentation of Christianity, but its thoughts and methods thenceforth controlled Greek dogmatic development." His *Against Celsus* was "the keenest and most convincing defense of the Christian faith that the ancient world brought forth." These and the more than six hundred other works credited to him by his contemporaries established him as the most prolific and creative Christian writer between Paul and Augustine.

He was also a pioneer in the historical and textual study of the Bible. With the help of his students in Caesarea he compared the many, slightly different New Testament texts then existing, hoping to determine from them what the original wording was. Moreover, he applied his scholarly mind to the Old Testament text, and after twenty years of prodigious labor he and his associates produced the famous *Hexapla*. This is a milestone in textual criticism. It presented six versions of the Old Testament for comparison and study. Each page of the *Hexapla* was divided into six columns. The first column gave the Hebrew text that Origen had obtained from his Jewish teachers; the second column offered this Hebrew text transliterated into Greek letters; the third, fourth, and sixth columns reproduced the different Greek translations of Aquila, Symmachus, and Theodotion; finally, the fifth column contained Origen's own critical text of the Septuagint.

Almost impossible to reproduce in its entirety because it occupied 6,500 pages, the *Hexapla* remained in Origen's library in Caesarea where Christian scholars consulted it for the next four hundred years. It perished in the 7th century during the Moslem conquest of Palestine. In view of the discovery in 1947 of the Dead Sea Scrolls, some of them found in jars in a cave not far from Jericho, it is interesting to note that in his discussion of Origen's work the 4th-century historian Eusebius says, "in the case of one of these [editions of the Psalms used in the *Hexapla*] he [Origen] has indicated again that it was found at Jericho in a jar in the time of Antoninus the son of Severus [or c. 211]."

Part Three

The Triumph of the Church A.D. 300-500

Chapter 10 **Christianity Becomes the Religion of the Roman Empire**

By the beginning of the 4th century Christianity, despite persecution, emerged as a vital force in the state. In its earliest days it had appealed mainly to the poor and uneducated. When the high quality of Christian lives became evident, however, and well-educated men of outstanding intellect began to interpret the gospel to their contemporaries, people of the upper classes, such as senatorial families, army officers, provincial governors, and members of the imperial family, adopted the new faith. The Christian communities established in all the major cities of the Mediterranean world attracted growing numbers of people, and churches were founded even in remote parts of the empire.

In his book, *Christianity*, Edwyn Bevan writes:

> It can hardly be doubted that the attraction of Christianity from the very beginning was social. It was not through a disembodied truth uttered into the air that the Christian "Good News" laid hold of men; it was through the corporate life of the little Christian societies in the cities of the ancient world. . . . Men coming into contact with such a group felt an atmosphere unlike anything else.

In a world of cruelty Christians were kind. In a social system based on rigid class divisions Christians regarded each person as a child of God. In a society permeated by loose sexual morals Christians tried to lead pure lives and their family life was guided by high ideals. They believed marriage to be indissoluble and the training of their children in Christian conduct to be one of their chief duties. In a period of change resulting in economic chaos Christians cared for widows and orphans, for the poor, the sick, the infirm. They extended hospitality to strangers of all ranks and races because they believed that the church was a world-wide society open to all. One pagan, impressed by the quality of Christian fellowship, exclaimed, "Behold, how these Christians love one another!" Christian people were generally honest, reliable, and good. They made their neighborhoods better places for everyone. Pagan Romans, disillusioned with their dying religion and alarmed by the slow disintegration of their civilization, inevitably flocked to the Christian churches. There they found themselves members of a group that claimed citizenship in heaven—a group whose faith and hope endowed life with meaning.

Tertullian, c. 200, with his characteristic precision, described the church at its best in his *Apology*:

> We are a society, with a common religious feeling, unity of discipline, a common bond of hope. We meet . . . to approach God in prayer. . . . We pray also for emperors, for their ministers and those in authority, for the security of the world, for peace on earth. . . . We meet to read the books of God . . . with those holy words we feed our faith.

The roll call of three church councils provides evidence of the outreach of Christianity in the West. Eighty-seven North African bishops attended the synod convened in 256 at Carthage. Nineteen bishops and twenty-four presbyters from all parts of Spain assembled in 305 at Elvira (Grenada).

Christianity Becomes the Religion of the Roman Empire

Nine years later, at Arles in southeast Gaul, thirty-three bishops, including three British bishops from Londinium (London), Eboracum (York), and possibly Lindum Colonia (Lincoln or Colchester) were present at the first general council of the Western church.

Until 311, however, Christianity remained an illegal religion with the threat of extreme punishment hanging over individual Christians. Diocletian's successor, Galerius, in an effort to retain the support of his non-Christian army, instituted the final persecution of the church. But on his deathbed the emperor abruptly reversed his policy and signed the Edict of Toleration, which gave Christians "the right to exist again and to set up their places of worship." The edict further stated that Christians should "pray to God for our recovery"—a possible indication that the dying emperor's personal concern was the compelling reason for issuing the law.

Twenty-three-year-old Constantine, a sub-emperor under Galerius and a ruler ambitious for supreme power, co-signed Galerius' Edict of 311. He strictly enforced its provisions, thereby winning enthusiastic support from the Christians. Constantine had already been acclaimed the successor to his father, the co-emperor Constantius, by the Roman garrison stationed at York. To win his empire young Constantine first had to overcome powerful rivals. After Galerius died, he led his troops across the Alps and south toward Rome to wrest control from Maxentius, emperor of the West. At the Milvian bridge over the Tiber north of Rome, Maxentius' superior force blocked Constantine's crossing of the river. According to Constantine's friend the Christian historian Eusebius, on the eve of the battle against Maxentius, Constantine beheld in a vision "a cross of light in the heavens" and a fiery inscription proclaiming, *In hoc signo vinces,* "By this sign you will conquer." Before joining battle the next morning Constantine had the Christian monogram, the Chi-Rho [☧] , hastily painted on his helmet and on the shields of his soldiers, many of whom undoubtedly were already Christians. They fought with zeal and Constantine was victorious. Maxentius drowned in the Tiber, leaving Constantine supreme in the West. The battle at the Milvian bridge on October 28, 312, marked a turning point in Christian history, for his victory won under the sign of the cross convinced Constantine that the God of the Christians was on his side and that his triumph was the reward of Christian faith.

In 313 when Constantine went to Milan for the marriage of his sister Constantia to Licinius, emperor of the East, the two emperors issued the joint Edict of Milan. It magnanimously stated that:

> Christians and all others should have freedom to follow the kind of religion they favored. . . . They are to be permitted to continue therein without any let or hindrance, and are not to be in any way troubled or molested. . . . It accords with the good order of the realm and the peacefulness of our times that each should have freedom to worship God after his own choice.

Relations between East and West became strained when Licinius resumed his former persecution of Christians. In the war that broke out in 323 between the two emperors Licinius was defeated and executed. Constantine now became sole ruler of the entire Roman world, both East and West.

Realizing that his immense empire needed some strong spiritual center in order to achieve unity, he discarded the old Roman gods and enlisted Christianity in the service of the state. Because he was impressed by the vitality and cohesion of the Christian communities and their moral superiority over other religious groups, he hoped to introduce Christian virtues into the life of the empire. He therefore acted rapidly to enhance the power and prestige of the church and to make it capable of supporting his absolutism. He appointed Christian bishops and clergy to his entourage; engaged Christian teachers for his sons; ordered his coins to be stamped with Christian symbols; encouraged his mother, Helena, to visit the Holy Land; and wore in the visor of his helmet one of the nails of the True Cross that she is said to have discovered in Jerusalem. He became a great patron of the church and adopted Christian principles in his humane laws, but some of his acts, such as the murder of his son and his first wife, are difficult to reconcile with his conversion to Christianity.

Partly because Rome remained the stronghold of the old dying Roman religion, Constantine moved his capital to Byzantium on the shores of the Bosphorus. In 330 he invited Christian bishops to dedicate to the Blessed Virgin this new city later called Constantinople. Here and in Rome, Jerusalem, Bethlehem, and other places, he directed imperial architects and artists to build and decorate splendid basilicas for Christian worship.

For the fifty new churches of Constantinople, he asked his friend Eusebius, bishop of Caesarea and author of *Historia Ecclesiastica,* to have fifty large copies of the Bible made. Constantine instructed Eusebius to have these copies transcribed by professional scribes using the most reliable master text available. They were to write on the best quality of vellum, not on perishable papyrus. The emperor further specified that the codices should be easy to read and convenient to carry. When completed in Caesarea they were to be brought to Constantinople in two public "carriages" under the care of a deacon.

The two finest Greek manuscript Bibles surviving from the first half of the 4th century, the Codex Vaticanus in the Vatican Library, Rome, and the Codex Sinaiticus in the British Library, London, may be two of the imperial copies.

The handwriting of these codices not only indicates the early 4th-century date of their origin but reveals that the scribe of the New Testament portion of the Codex Vaticanus probably also copied part of the Codex Sinaiticus. The New Testament canon had evidently not been completely established when these Bibles were made, because, as was noted above, the Codex Sinaiticus contains the *Epistle of Barnabas* and the *Shepherd of Hermas,* both later excluded from the canon.

Constantine, becoming alarmed that the dispute over Arianism (*see* Chapter 11) might destroy the unity of the church, involved himself in this question of Christian belief and convened in 325 the first ecumenical church council. It met in northern Asia Minor in the city of Nicaea. Constantine himself presided over its opening session in all his imperial splendor, apparently determined to assert a supremacy in church affairs to which his traditional Roman title *Pontifex Maximus* seemed to entitle him.

Throughout his reign Constantine was technically not a Christian but remained a catechumen, or candidate for baptism under instruction, postponing his baptism until he was on his deathbed. In this way he believed he could be assured of dying with all his sins forgiven. He died in 337 and was buried in the Church of the Apostles in Constantinople, where he had prepared his own tomb in the midst of memorials to the Apostles.

Constantine's sons continued his religious policies. After their deaths his nephew Julian, known as "the Apostate" (361-363), became the last Roman emperor openly to practice paganism. Though he tried to restore the worship of the old gods and revoke Christian privileges, he failed. Before his death he is reported to have exclaimed, "Thou hast conquered, O Galilean!" Finally, in 392, when Theodosius I prohibited pagan rites and made it unlawful for people to hold beliefs contrary to those of the church,

Christianity became the only legal religion of the empire.

The church's triumph brought with it new problems. The quality of church life declined when crowds of pagans, desiring the special privileges granted to Christians, presented themselves as candidates for baptism and became Christians in name only. Moreover, the power of the church over its own affairs was undermined when the eastern emperors, beginning with Constantine, not only interfered in ecclesiastical matters but used the church to implement state policies.

Chapter 11 The Creed and the Scriptures

Survival had been the church's most urgent problem during its first centuries, but when the state accepted the church, a new concern became paramount. This was controversy over beliefs. Keen Greek minds trying to penetrate the mystery of Christ and the meaning of the earliest creed of apostolic times, "Jesus is Lord" (1 Corinthians 12.3), introduced new doctrines. The creed, which had developed in Rome in the 2nd century and was later known as the Apostles' Creed, had effectively ruled out the Gnostic heresy. By the 4th century, however, a radically new doctrine was introduced by Arius, a devout and learned priest of advanced years who was highly regarded as a preacher.

In his church in Alexandria, Arius taught that Christ, as a created being, is subordinate to God the Father, being neither fully God nor fully man. For this teaching Arius and his sympathizers were condemned by the patriarch of Alexandria. Many Greek theologians saw that Arius' doctrine diluted the Christian faith and made of Christ virtually a half-god, in many respects similar to the gods of the pagans.

The opposition to Arius' new doctrine was led by Athanasius, a brilliant young deacon soon to become patriarch of Alexandria. Athanasius was convinced that Christ is truly God and fully man and that his is the one life in which the nature of God is completely revealed. This faith was founded on the Scriptures (John 1.1-18; Colossians 1.15-20; Hebrews 1.1-4; etc.). To this discerning Greek thinker, Arianism offered no basis for the salvation of humanity. Accordingly, Athanasius wrote that Christ "was made

The Creed and the Scriptures

man that we might be made divine," a statement partly derived from Paul's words that "in him [Christ] the whole fulness of deity dwells bodily, and you have come to fulness of life in him . . ." (Colossians 2.9).

The controversy narrowed itself to two phrases. The party headed by Athanasius maintained that Christ is "of *one* substance [*homoousion*] with the Father." Against this, the Arians argued that Christ is "of *like* substance, or essence [*homoiousion*], with the Father." Some people, impatient with the subtleties of Greek thought, dismissed the whole matter as a quarrel over a syllable. Even Constantine wrote that it seemed "of a truly insignificant character and quite unworthy of such fierce contention."

Nevertheless, the emperor recognized that the dispute threatened the unity of the church on which he had staked the well-being of his empire. Accordingly, as was noted above, he convened a council of church leaders at Nicaea in Asia Minor, paid the traveling expenses of the more than three hundred bishops who attended, and presided over the opening session. His friend Eusebius was present and noted that many of the attending bishops still bore the marks of the tortures they had suffered during the recent persecutions of Diocletian and Galerius. The almost unanimous vote of the bishops at Nicaea to reject the Arian creed was in part a reflection of the emperor's wish to unify the church. The council deposed and banished Arius and the two bishops who sided with him.

Before the Council of Nicaea adjourned, a small group led by Athanasius insisted that an authoritative statement of the church's faith be drawn up and approved. This was the origin of the so-called Nicene Creed, the first universal creed of the entire church. It described Christ as "very God of very God," of the same divine essence as God the Father, who for our salvation was incarnated in human flesh and became man. This creed, revised by the Council of Constantinople in 381 and endorsed at Chalcedon by the Fourth Ecumenical Council in 451, expresses the basic conviction of the church that Christ is a complete revelation of God in terms of a genuine human life. It was adopted by both the Eastern Orthodox and the Roman Catholic churches, and later by most Protestant churches, as the explanation of the mystery of Christ's nature and person. In the East, Christological disputes did not end with the adoption of the Nicene Creed, for Arianism and later Nestorianism and Monophysitism continued to provoke bitter controversies.

Athanasius' name is not only associated with the Nicene Creed but with the canon of the New Testament. As was mentioned earlier, his Easter letter of 367 to the clergy of Alexandria contains the earliest-known list of the twenty-seven books of the New Testament canon.

Athanasius, and Eastern Christians in general, read the New Testament in its original language, Greek. Their Old Testament was, of course, the Septuagint. In the West, where Latin had become the language of the state and the church, several Latin translations circulated. Because these Old Latin versions, as they are called, were without literary distinction, the 4th-century pope Damasus commissioned his secretary, Jerome, to revise and correct them.

Jerome (340-420) was not only a Biblical scholar of vast learning but had a flare for languages, wrote a pure, incisive Latin, and was expert in the use of the telling phrase. Even Jerome, however, had misgivings about translating. As he wrote to the pope, people accustomed to one or another version of the Scriptures would "call me a sacrilegious forger for daring to add something to the ancient books or to make corrections in them." Nevertheless, he decided "to search out the truth," and he undertook his task of correcting the mistakes of inaccurate translators and the changes of ignorant critics and half-awake copyists.

Retiring to a monastery near Bethlehem where he enlisted

The Creed and the Scriptures 47

The Frick Collection, New York

Saint Jerome—El Greco (1541-1614)

With dramatic intensity, El Greco portrays this outstanding fourth-century Biblical scholar wearing the robes of a cardinal and pointing to a copy of his Latin translation of the Bible, known as the Vulgate.

the help of Jewish scholars, he translated the Hebrew text of the Old Testament into Latin. He also revised the Old Latin versions of the New Testament, correcting them from contemporary Greek codices. In translating, he tried to reproduce the meaning of the original text rather than to render the equivalent of each word.

The success of the new translation, completed about A.D. 400 and eventually known as the Vulgate, was not immediate. Some readers who had become accustomed to the archaic phraseology of the Old Latin versions accused Jerome of making heretical changes. Augustine, the great bishop of Hippo, wrote to Jerome that when a certain bishop in North Africa read from the new version, its strangeness provoked his congregation to riot. Jerome replied that these people probably disliked the fact that he had used *hedera* (ivy) in place of the more familiar *cucurbita* (gourd) for the vine under which Jonah found shelter. In his reply to Augustine, Jerome admitted that, after all, he did not think that *ivy* was a good translation.

Augustine himself was not fully satisfied with the common everyday language of Jerome's version. As a youth immersed in classical literature he had disdained the crudeness of the Old Latin versions, though later, as a Christian, he said he preferred them to the new translation because they conveyed a sense of the antiquity of the Bible and the long continuity of the faith.

Despite its critics, the Vulgate was, for its time, a significant and scholarly achievement that eventually earned wide recognition. It was adopted everywhere and remained *the* Bible of Western Europe for a thousand years.

From his years of translating the Bible, Jerome perceived that its deepest meanings do not lie on the surface. "Everything in the Sacred Books shines and glistens, even in its outer shell," wrote Jerome, "but its marrow is sweeter; if you want the kernel, you must break the shell."

Augustine, doubtless remembering his inability to understand the Scriptures and his scorn of them during his pagan youth, declared that only within the life of the Christian community could the Bible be truly understood. The aim of all Bible reading and study, he said, was to increase a person's faith, hope, and love. Furthermore, he believed that the primary reason for expounding the Scriptures was not to display scholarly brilliance, much less to dazzle an audience, but to help people understand their faith and develop Christian virtues.

Chapter 12 **New Churches and Enriched Worship**

When Christianity became the state religion, its most visible change occurred in its buildings. The house-churches of the apostolic age (Colossians 4.15) and the small, unobtrusive churches in which Christians had worshiped during the years of persecution were gradually replaced by large, stately edifices often built with imperial patronage. They were planned to accommodate the crowds of pagans who presented themselves for baptism or who came to hear the great preachers. These new churches provided scope for more impressive ceremonies and liturgy.

As early as 323 Constantine built the Basilica of the Savior in Rome, where now the Church of St. John Lateran stands. As the new basilica adjoined the palace of Plautius Lateranus, which had been given by the emperor to Pope Sylvester I, it became the cathedral of Rome and was called "the Mother and Head of all the churches *Urbis et Orbis* (of the city and of the world)." Constantine's Roman architects built it on the basilica plan, which had been developed for Roman law courts and imperial audience halls. The emperor endowed it with chalices, bowls, and chandeliers of silver and gold.

The next year, according to tradition, Constantine built another basilica, this one on Vatican Hill at the site of St. Peter's tomb. This was the first St. Peter's, a church planned to accommodate forty thousand people standing in the customary attitude of prayer. It was a splendid structure with a forecourt, a long nave, five aisles, and a forest of columns crowned with sumptuous capitals. Paintings and mosaics adorned its walls. When it fell into ruin the site was cleared for the present St. Peter's. Work was begun on it in 1506 and continued under such artists as Bramante, Raphael, Michelangelo, and Bernini.

Constantine's building projects did not end with his two great basilicas in Rome. Under imperial authority Bishop Macarius of Jerusalem excavated beneath the Roman forum of the Holy City and uncovered a rocky cavern that he identified as Christ's tomb. Knowledge of this site as the place of the resurrection may have been handed down to successive generations of Christians after Jerusalem was destroyed in A.D. 70, following which Roman structures were built on the ruins. Constantine instructed Macarius to erect a worthy memorial at this most holy place. The emperor's mother, Helena, arrived in Jerusalem at this time and was undoubtedly shown plans for the projected group of buildings at Christ's sepulcher. She herself had two basilicas built elsewhere, one on the Mount of Olives and the second in Bethlehem.

The chief buildings Constantine ordered for Jerusalem consisted of a great domed, circular structure over Christ's tomb and a basilica. Greek Christians called the circular building the *Anastasis*, meaning "Resurrection." Latin Christians referred to it as the Holy Sepulcher. Remains of it are preserved in the rotunda of the crusaders' 12th-century church, parts of which exist today. Near the Anastasis a vast basilica was erected whose interior surface, according to Eusebius, "was hidden beneath panels of polychrome marble. . . . The ceiling was ornamented by sculptured panels let into it which resembled a huge sea . . . and in which the brilliant golden decorations spread a thousand sparks over the temple."

After Constantine's complex of buildings in Jerusalem was solemnly dedicated in 335, crowds of pilgrims came to worship at Christendom's holiest site. Among those who left records of their impressions was the anonymous "Pilgrim of Bordeaux." He saw the basilica in the course of construction in 333. A half century later, the shrewdly observant Etheria, or Egeria, a great Spanish lady as well as a sincere and pious Christian, visited all the holy places, with her Bible in hand. Her letters, discovered in 1884, carefully describe the religious ceremonies she attended, thus establishing an invaluable record of the liturgy in the 4th century. She also comments on the impressive interior of the Church of the Holy Sepulcher with its gold and silver decorations, its curtains, jewels, candles, and lampstands.

The most imposing of the early churches is Justinian's Church of Hagia Sophia, a name meaning "Holy Wisdom" and denoting the Person of Christ. This structure still survives after earthquakes and several rebuildings. It was erected in Constantinople by the architects Anthemios of Tralles and Isidoros of Melitus. At its dedication in 537 the Emperor Justinian is reported to have exclaimed, "Solomon, I have surpassed you!" It stood as a symbol of the emperor's attempt, following the Gothic invasions of Italy, to strengthen the church as a bulwark of the state and to revive a universal Christian Roman Empire. As the imperial church, it remained the political and religious center of the Eastern Empire until the 15th century. Its four massive stone piers and their arches, together with half-domes and monolithic columns of marble and porphyry, all support and buttress an enormous main dome that seems to float, like a golden shell, one hundred and eighty feet above the pavement of the immense interior. Polychrome marbles and golden mosaics decorate the walls and ceilings of this building, which represents the supreme achievement of Byzantine architecture. As Hagia Sophia was the cathedral church of the patriarch, his silver throne was placed in the apse. When the Turks captured Constantinople in 1453, the church was transformed into a mosque. Today it is used as a museum of Byzantine art.

In the sumptuous new churches and in humbler ones everywhere, prayer and worship echoed with the thoughts and words of the Bible. These time-honored expressions of man's life in God not only gave depth and eloquence to Christian devotion but also fostered unity of spirit in the prayer life of the entire church. People everywhere drew inspiration from the Bible. It nourished Christian hope; it gave substance to Christian faith. The scriptural record of God's revelation of himself in creation, in Israel's history, and finally in Jesus Christ, gave assurance of the truth of Christianity. Christian people and their leaders, from their study of the Bible, gained a deeper understanding of the range of Christ's gospel.

Impressive baptismal ceremonies in the new churches initiated adult candidates into their full Christian life. Handsome structures, like the Baptistry in Ravenna, were built and lavishly decorated for this purpose. Irenaeus mentioned infant baptism as early as 185, but this custom did not become widespread until the 6th century, by which time most adults had been brought up in Christian families.

Regular services of worship were conducted on Sundays, the day of Christ's resurrection. At these services the men occupied one side of the church and the women the other, according to the old synagogue custom. Youths stood or sat in a group by themselves. Seats were provided for old people; women with children were given a special place. Deacons watched over these arrangements and prevented anyone from whispering, laughing, or sleeping.

The Sunday service was in two parts. The first, which was open to everyone, began with the chanting of psalms and the reading of portions of the Old Testament, the letters of Paul and other apostles, and the Gospels. The Scripture selection was then interpreted in the light of Christ's teachings, a procedure borrowed from synagogue practice (Luke 4.16-21). Prayers, often a sermon, and finally a benediction ended this part of the service. Those who had not yet been baptized were then dismissed.

The portions of Scripture read at the Sunday service were chosen with the aim of completing the reading of the Bible during a certain period of time. By the end of the 4th century the Christian church, following Jewish custom, had developed lectionaries and had compiled lists of readings appropriate for such special seasons as Holy Week, Easter, Pentecost, the Nativity, and the Epiphany.

The most sacred part of Christian worship, the Lord's Supper, began when the non-baptized left the church and only the communicants remained. After a deacon said, "*Kyrie Eleison*" (The Lord have mercy), the people made the responses in a litany and recited the creed and the Lord's Prayer. Then the bishop, in a festal garment with the priests around him, celebrated the Lord's Supper, which was called the Eucharist. This name, from the Greek *eucharistia* (thanksgiving), emphasized thanksgiving for Christ's incarnation and sacrificial death and for the new life he imparts to his people. The church, believing in the sacramental presence of Christ in the bread and the wine, repeated his words establishing the life-giving mystery, "This is my body which is for you. . . . This cup is the new covenant in my blood" (1 Corinthians 11.24-25, cf. Mark 14.22-24).

Chapter 13 Prominent Preachers and Leaders

During the great age of preachers, from the late 4th century to the middle of the 5th, sermons became an important feature of the Sunday service in various cities. Usually the bishop was the preacher. He would explain the Scriptures and apply their teachings to daily life. Often the congregation responded to his most effective points by applauding. Among the outstanding preachers of this period were three bishops: John Chrysostom of the Eastern Church, and Ambrose and Augustine of the Western.

John Chrysostom (c. 345-407), a scholarly priest of ascetic habits and the greatest of the Greek Fathers, was given the name Chrysostom, meaning "golden-mouthed," because of his eloquence as a preacher. He interpreted the Bible, not in the allegorical manner then popular, but from a literal and historical point of view. The Scriptures, he declared, are the tools of a Christian. He suggested that a family invite the neighbors in to read the Bible with them. He used to announce the Scriptural passage on which he would base his next Sunday's sermon, so that his people could study it at home and come prepared to understand his message. His sermons on the practical issues of Christian life were so successful that for twelve years he remained Antioch's favorite preacher. Once he rebuked his congregation for applauding his sermon, criticizing their action as unseemly, but they applauded him all the more for his rebuke! Because of his great fame, the emperor, in 398, called him to be patriarch of Constantinople. There, as in Antioch, crowds hung upon his sermons. Nevertheless, his attempts to reform the careless lives of his clergy and his disapproval of women's extravagance in dress, which the Empress Eudoxia believed to be aimed at herself, angered the clergy as well as the empress. They secretly convened an illegal synod that condemned and deposed the patriarch on false charges and exiled him to Armenia. In protest, Pope Innocent I withdrew from communion with Constantinople, but John Chrysostom died in exile.

Ambrose (c. 337-397), educated in Rome for a civil career, became governor of Milan at an early age. When a tumult arose there over the election of a new bishop, the young governor, hoping to quiet the angry crowd, entered the church. While he spoke, a cry rang out and was taken up by the whole assembly, "Ambrose, bishop!" Though he was not yet baptized, he interpreted his election by acclamation as a call from God and prepared, through baptism and ordination to the ministry, for his consecration as bishop. He gave his money to the poor and his lands to the church and devoted himself to the study of theology. Personal integrity combined with intelligence and a talent for administration made him one of the foremost churchmen of the West.

His theological writings, mostly on practical matters of Christian ethics, reveal his wide classical as well as his Scriptural learning. From his deep sense of sin and grace, he wrote, "I will not glory because I am righteous, but I will glory because I am redeemed. I will not glory because I am free from sin, but because my sins are forgiven." Of the Bible he said, "As in Paradise, God walks in the Holy Scriptures, seeking man. When a sinner reads these Scriptures, he hears God's voice saying, 'Adam where art thou?'"

For his cathedral in Milan, Ambrose arranged psalms to be sung antiphonally by the congregation. He wrote in four-line metrical stanzas some of the first Christian hymns, a few of which are found in modern hymnals. He also introduced plain song, an unharmonized melody in free rhythm, possibly derived from ancient Hebrew and Greek singing. In Milan plain song is still sung under the name Ambrosian chant.

His greatest triumph occurred when he confronted Emperor Theodosius the Great at the door of his cathedral. Ambrose forbade the emperor to enter until he had openly confessed guilt for his punitive massacre of the people of Thessalonica and had asked God to forgive him. In complying with this demand, the emperor, in effect, acknowledged the supremacy of the bishop's spiritual authority and his right to intervene in secular affairs.

Among Ambrose's many gifts was his eloquence as a preacher. It was this that originally attracted Augustine to him, but finally the great bishop's message touched his heart, quickening his resolve to become a Christian.

Augustine (354-430) was born in North Africa of a pagan father and a Christian mother named Monica. Although as a young man he lived mainly for enjoyment, seizing every pleasure life offers, he continued to be haunted by a desire to discover the true meaning of life. To that end he turned to the Bible, only to be repelled by its style, which, as was noted above, he found inferior to his favorite Latin and Greek authors. He became a teacher of rhetoric, first in Rome and later in Milan. There he came under the spell of Ambrose's preaching. After his baptism by the great bishop in 387, he was transformed by his Christian experience and returned to North Africa. He devoted the rest of his life to the service of God as Biblical scholar, writer, priest, and bishop of Hippo. He died while Hippo was besieged by the Vandals.

Though Augustine's influence on Christian thought was second only to that of Paul, in his own day his basic doctrines of sin and grace were challenged. The learned British, or perhaps Irish, monk and theologian, Pelagius, went to Rome about 400 and preached a new doctrine that denied original sin. Pelagius taught that men and women by their own efforts can bring about their own salvation; they can perfect themselves by faith and good works alone. In 415 Augustine wrote to Jerome, then presiding over his monastery in Bethlehem, warning him that Pelagius planned to introduce his heresy in the East. Jerome wrote unkindly of Pelagius, calling him "a dolt of dolts, with his wits dulled by a surfeit of his native Scotch porridge." Pelagianism was condemned, but the questions of free will and grace that Pelagius raised still remain.

Despite challenges like these, Augustine's influence in his own day and in subsequent periods was immense. Unceasingly he wrote letters, treatises, books, and sermons. Five hundred of the latter still survive. Two of his books influenced Western Christendom profoundly and remain religious classics: his *Confessions* and his *De Civitate Dei* (City of God). The former, written about the year 400, is a spiritual autobiography expressing a deeper level of personal devotion than that of any other writer since Paul. In its opening prayer occurs the sentence, "Thou has made us for Thyself, and our hearts are restless until they find their rest in Thee."

Taking his title from Psalm 87.2, Augustine began to write his *City of God* in 412. Only two years before, Alaric king of the Visigoths had penetrated Rome's defenses and, with his fierce warriors, captured the hitherto impregnable imperial city. This incredible event shocked thoughtful people everywhere and produced fear that it was the prelude to the approaching end of history. Many, seeking a scapegoat for the catastrophe, accused the church of having brought about Rome's fall by causing the abandonment of the old gods who had heretofore protected the city. Augustine, however, placed the event in perspective and cited evidence from the Scriptures for a philosophy of history that restored faith in God and gave meaning to the entire sweep of the human drama. Earthly powers come and go, he declared, but the city of God, which is the church and the refuge and true home of mankind, endures forever. In medieval times both church and empire drew inspiration from Augustine's dream of the city of God on earth. It is reported that Charlemagne used to sleep with a copy of this book beneath his pillow.

Chapter 14 The Beginnings of Monasticism

Monasticism appeared and grew rapidly after Christianity was recognized by the state in the 4th century. At this time, when great numbers of pagans flocked into the church, it found itself more and more entangled in worldly affairs. Partly in reaction against these mundane concerns, but basically because Christians from the beginning had renounced material values to gain spiritual rewards, men and women dedicated their lives to God in devotion and asceticism.

Anthony (c. 250-350), a wealthy young Egyptian, is usually regarded as the founder of Christian monasticism. After listening to the Gospel selection read in church one day, he literally obeyed Jesus' words, "Go, sell what you have, and give to the poor, and you will have treasure in heaven; and come, follow me" (Mark 10.21). Eventually Anthony retired to the desert where in solitude he prayed, practiced austerities, and fought against temptation. Many men, inspired by his holiness, which was in sharp contrast to the wickedness of the world, followed him into the desert. They lived alone in caves as hermits but often worshiped and ate together. As leader of this colony of monks, Anthony acquired the name Abbot. Most of the monks in his community, being illiterate, memorized the Scriptures so that they could meditate on them day and night. Athanasius, patriarch of Alexandria, after hiding with these hermit monks during one of his banishments, became so impressed with their devotion and way of life that he wrote a biography of their founder, thus spreading the fame of

Anthony Abbot and informing the church about the new movement.

Pachomius (292-346), an Egyptian soldier who became a Christian, introduced a new form of monasticism in which the monks did not live as hermits but in a close-knit association under a definite and very severe rule. They performed assigned tasks, kept regular hours of worship, and wore similar dress. Large numbers of men and women were attracted to this cenobite, or community, type of monasticism, making it the preferred form. Ten monasteries were established in Egypt by the middle of the 4th century. Pachomius' sister founded two religious communities for women.

As early as c. 362 Martin of Tours, famous for sharing his military cloak with One whom he assumed to be a beggar, established a monastery near Poitiers in Gaul and became an advocate of monasticism.

Jerome worked on his Bible translations while directing a monastery in Bethlehem. He also supervised a nearby convent for nuns built by the wealthy Roman matron Paula and her daughter. Renaissance artists often depicted Jerome at his desk in a cell, with the lion of his legend sitting, or sleeping, at his feet.

Basil (c. 330-379), bishop of Caesarea in Cappadocia and one of the outstanding interpreters of the Nicene Creed, modified Pachomius' cenobite type of monasticism by introducing normal occupations and a more wholesome atmosphere into the ascetic life. According to his Rule the monastic day was divided into eight periods of common worship. These were interspersed with study of the Scriptures and manual labor or other useful work, such as the education of children. Macrina, the saintly sister of both Basil of Caesarea and Gregory of Nyssa and herself an outstanding theologian, is credited with founding women's conventual life.

Chapter 15 The Expansion of the Church

From its earliest days the church had obeyed Christ's command to carry his good news "to the end of the earth" (Acts 1.8). Long before Constantine issued the Edict of Milan, Christian missionaries had penetrated to the far reaches of the Roman Empire and beyond. As has been noted, by the end of the 2nd century the gospel had been preached in Roman Britain; Alban, the earliest British martyr, died in Diocletian's persecutions; and three British bishops attended the Council of Arles in 314.

At the other end of the Christian axis, Armenia, a vassal kingdom under the Roman Empire, was the first country to adopt Christianity as its official religion. Gregory, called the Illuminator, converted and baptized King Tiridates in 301. This was eleven years before Constantine fought at the Milvian bridge under banners bearing Christian symbols.

North of the Danube many of the Visigoths were converted by one of their own people, Ulfilas (c. 311-383), called the "apostle to the Goths." He had become a Christian, possibly in Constantinople, and was consecrated a missionary bishop in 341. As the Gothic language had never before been written, Ulfilas had to design a Gothic alphabet from Greek and Latin letters before recording his Gothic translation of the Scriptures. A similar situation faced the learned priest Mestrop in Armenia in the 5th century. He too had to invent an alphabet in order to provide the Armenian Church with its own translation of the Bible. (From his comprehensive study of Christian history, Kenneth Scott Latourette concludes that, "More languages have been reduced to writing by Christian missionaries than by all other agencies put together.")

Because Ulfilas venerated the sacred text, he translated it literally, almost word for word, but, being critical of the spirit of the Books of Kings, he declined to translate them lest they arouse the warlike passions of his people. A splendid 6th-century manuscript of Ulfilas' Gothic translation of the Gospels, the Codex Argenteus, written in silver and gold on purple parchment, is preserved in the University of Uppsala, Sweden.

Through the labors of such missionaries as Ulfilas, many of the Visigoths, Ostrogoths, Vandals, Burgundians, and Lombards were Christians when they moved across the borders of the empire during the great tribal migrations. Even the non-Christian tribes had little difficulty in forsaking their pagan gods when they settled among the old Roman populations, for to them civilization and Christianity seemed synonymous and they eagerly adopted both.

The Celtic tribes of Ireland, with their long history of paganism, were introduced to Christianity by Patrick (c. 389-461), a third-generation British Christian. During his youth, Patrick was captured by Irish raiders on his father's estate, which was possibly in Wales, and was carried to heathen Ireland. There he spent six years as a slave tending his master's sheep. By his own account, he prayed "a hundred prayers a day and nearly as many at night, staying out in the woods or on the mountain." One night, in a dream, he heard a voice saying, "Your ship is ready," and, fleeing to the coast, he persuaded a shipowner to take him home. Before long he heard Irish voices that seemed to plead with him, saying, "Holy boy, come back and walk among us once more." After receiving training in a monastery in Gaul, Patrick was consecrated a missionary bishop in 432 and returned to Ireland. There he converted the chiefs of clans, established dioceses, and was especially successful in founding monasteries on land donated by the chiefs. After his twenty-nine years of missionary work, Ireland could be called a Christian region.

At the age of about fifteen, Clovis (466-511) succeeded to the kingship of the Salian Franks and led his Germanic tribe to victory over the Romans in northern and central Gaul. Soon he united all the Franks under his rule. His wife, Clotilda, a Burgundian princess belonging to the Roman rather than the Arian communion, persuaded her husband to embrace her Christian faith. Accordingly, on Christmas Day, 496, the king and three thousand of his followers were baptized at Rheims. Because this won for Clovis the good will of the old Roman population and the support of its bishops, he was able to extend his realm from the Rhine to the Pyrenees at the expense of the Germanic tribes who had been converted by followers of Arius. Clovis thus became the founder of France. At Paris, his capital, he built the Church of the Holy Apostles, later known as the Church of St. Genevieve. The fact that the predominant Franks belonged to the orthodox, or Roman, communion influenced other Germanic tribes to abandon their former Arianism and become orthodox Christians also, thus giving Western Europe a greater degree of unity than it might otherwise have attained.

In the two centuries from 300 to 500, as these representative stories indicate, the church advanced on many fronts, so that by the beginning of the Middle Ages it had begun to convert the barbarians and to move into positions of authority and power.

Part Four
The Middle Ages
A.D. 500-1500

Chapter 16   The Church Survives the Breakdown of the Empire

By the 6th century the classical world of antiquity, having achieved a high degree of order and civilized living, had already lost its creative energy and was disintegrating. Under successive blows from invading peoples the carefully guarded frontiers of the Roman Empire crumbled as waves of barbarians pushed south and west across the Danube, the Rhine, and the North Sea, or rowed up the rivers deep into the unprotected countryside.

The great invasions began in the 5th century. Between 410 and 442 the withdrawal of the Roman legions from Britain after more than three hundred years of occupation left the Romanized population a prey to internal strife and to marauding bands of Irish from the west, Picts from the north, and Jutes, Angles, and Saxons from the east. In Italy, after Alaric and his Visigoths sacked Rome in 410, a new invader, the Huns led by Attila, approached the imperial city in 452. These fierce warriors from Central Asia would undoubtedly have taken Rome if Leo I, one of the greatest of the early popes, had not gone out to meet the barbarian chieftain. Somehow the pope persuaded Attila to withdraw. Leo's statesmanlike act greatly enhanced the prestige of his office, for it showed that when governors and generals abandoned their responsibilities, the church was ready to step into the vacuum left by the collapse of the civil power.

In the year 476, the traditional date of the "fall" of the Roman Empire, the Ostrogoths deposed the last Roman emperor of the West. In the East, though the Byzantine empire was attacked in the 6th century by the Persians, and in the 7th by the Moslems, it managed to endure for a millennium until it was finally overrun by the Turks in 1453.

In the West the vast movement of invading tribes brought such slaughter, confusion, and squalor that the early medieval period is often referred to as the Dark Ages. Some of the barbarians who came as settlers quickly adopted the ways of life they found in the coveted lands. Most of them, however, in their eagerness to appropriate the fruits of a high culture, laid heavy hands on whatever they desired, unwittingly destroying the delicate web of a civilization they took for granted but were unable either to understand or to maintain. Roads and harbors were neglected and fell into disrepair, thus interrupting communication and trade. People, in fear of the present and dreading the future, ceased to make long-range plans. Masons and other craftsmen no longer found employment building the enduring stone structures for which the Romans had been famous. Even the art of bricklaying disappeared when the only demand was for rude shelters. Aqueducts once broken remained in partial ruin. A city like Rome, in which a million or so people had once lived, shrank to about fifty thousand, owing in large part to its failing water supply.

Most disastrous of all, the great centers of learning in Rome, Alexandria, Carthage, and Milan were destroyed and their libraries burned. Under such conditions original scholarship and creative thought all but ceased. Education, except in the monasteries, disappeared and eventually few people, even among the clergy, were able to read or write.

The Church Survives the Breakdown of the Empire 67

In faulty Latin the half-illiterate Gregory, bishop of Tours in the 6th century, wrote, "Woe to our time, for the study of books has perished from among us."

During this period of chaos, while most of the great achievements of Greco-Roman times were being engulfed by barbarians and by ignorance, Christianity rescued all that could be saved of the dying civilization. The church, with its common creed and centralized authority under the bishop of Rome, was able to preserve many Roman ideas of order and to hold together some of the structure of empire. With its Bible and liturgy the church kept the Latin language alive and safeguarded some of the old scholarship and learning. To people living in an age of confusion and despair, the church preached of eternal peace and blessedness beyond the reach of lawlessness, whether political, economic, or social. Finally, the church was the source of the spiritual force that gave unity and strength to the new civilization. When the long period of disorder ended and relative stability reappeared, Christianity emerged as the standard-bearer of western civilization. The era in which this occurred could rightly be called the Age of Faith. Every town had its church; monasteries flourished; learning revived; and the cathedrals, which are still the most visible achievements of the Middle Ages, stood as massive stone symbols of the faith of kings, bishops, and common people that Christ's heavenly kingdom is a reality.

Chapter 17 Monasticism

After the breakdown of the Roman Empire, monasticism, which since its appearance in the 3rd and 4th centuries had been rooted in personal faith and whole-hearted devotion to Christ, became the main strength of the church. Though designed for single and solitary people, the monastic ideal profoundly influenced the lives of lay people as well. The monasteries afforded islands of relative security to men and women seeking refuge from the social and political turmoil of the Middle Ages. Nevertheless, the monasteries were far more than shelters. They fostered learning and education, and they trained missionary monks to carry the gospel to the barbarians. Because some of the monastic orders emphasized practical labor, and because many monasteries had to be self-supporting, they demonstrated how to cultivate the land and gain a living from it. Monks cleared and drained their acres, raised crops, established orchards and vineyards, raised cattle, sheep, and poultry, and pioneered in the best farming methods, all the while dignifying labor by performing it. They continued to exercise the responsible stewardship over nature enjoined in the first chapter of Genesis.

The credit for preserving much of the ancient classical learning belongs to the monasteries. Cassiodorus (480-575), a man of letters who was also a monk and a statesman, founded two monasteries on his family estates in southern Italy. At the end of his political career as secretary to Emperor Theodoric the Great, he retired to the monastery at Vivarium. There he collected a library, taught the monks to study and copy old manuscripts, and translated Greek books into Latin. He also revised Jerome's Latin Vulgate from the best obtainable manuscripts, for in the century and a half since its translation copyists' errors had corrupted the text. Such activities as these were undertaken in monasteries everywhere during the centuries of ignorance that engulfed Western Europe.

Benedict of Nursia (480-547), the great reformer of western monasticism and author of the Benedictine Rule, saved the monastic movement from excesses of asceticism and other unwise conditions. He founded, c. 529, the mother monastery of the Benedictine Order on the hill of Monte Cassino, midway between Rome and Naples. Here, after a trial year of monastery life, candidates took the monk's vow of poverty, chastity, and obedience and thereafter lived in community under an elected abbot. Though Benedict believed that worship was the monk's prime duty, he required study and labor in the fields and in the shops, warning that, "Idleness is the enemy of the soul." In the course of history the Benedictine Order contributed twenty-four popes, two hundred cardinals, and some fifteen thousand writers and scholars to the church.

Celtic monasticism differed from the more moderate and balanced Benedictine type in its highly mystical spirit and ascetic rigor. In the monasteries founded by Patrick after 432 the sons and daughters of the great Irish families often lived in clusters of wattle huts surrounded by earthen ramparts. There they enjoyed a measure of peace from almost continual tribal warfare.

The missionary activity and devotion to learning that characterized Irish monasticism can be traced to Finnian, who in c. 520 founded the monastery and school of Clonard. This became the prototype of other monasteries, such as those at Clonmacnois, Bangor, Derry, Durrow, and Kells. During the golden age of Irish monastic scholarship in the 6th and 7th centuries the monastic schools, with their broad curriculum of Latin, Greek, arithmetic, geometry, astronomy, geography, and music, attracted scholars from many parts of Europe and exercised an influence on the Carolingian revival of learning.

Finnian's pupil Columba, with twelve companions, set forth in frail, skin-covered curraghs for Scotland in 563 on an overseas mission. They landed near the west coast, on the island of Iona among the Inner Hebrides. There they established a monastery which became the center of Celtic Christianity and from which Columba and his monks evangelized Scotland and Northumbria. In Columba's biography written by Adamnan, a later abbot of Iona, occurs the first literary record of the Loch Ness monster. It is the story of how the creature threatened a swimmer, but retreated when Columba made the sign of the cross.

Aidan, a monk from Iona, established a monastery in 634 on the island of Lindisfarne off the northeast coast of England. From here Christianity spread throughout Northumbria where the recently arrived Anglo-Saxon invaders had extinguished virtually all traces of the earlier Roman Christianity. Irish monks also traveled to the continent, establishing St. Gall in Switzerland and Bobbio in North Italy, monasteries that became famous in the Middle Ages for their libraries and cultural life.

In Irish monasteries, where scribes continually copied manuscripts, the illumination of books developed into a high art. One of the finest examples of Celtic art is the *Book of Kells,* a manuscript of the Latin Gospels decorated with superb interlacing designs and fantastic human and animal forms. Probably created at Iona in the 8th or 9th century, but brought to Kells in Ireland at the time of the Viking raids, it is now in Trinity College Library, Dublin. Other illuminated manuscripts influenced by Celtic art include: the 7th-century *Book of Durrow,* which is also in the Trinity College Library; and the *Lindisfarne Gospels,* now in the British Library, London. The illuminations in the latter manuscript are of such beauty and intricacy that they were once thought to be the work, not of men, but of angels.

Outstanding among the monastery-trained English men and women who helped to carry the gospel to the continent was Winfrid, an Anglo-Saxon from Devonshire who was educated in a Benedictine monastery near Winchester. Pope Gregory II gave him the name of Boniface (c. 680-754). This "apostle of Germany," as he was called, worked under the protection of Charles Martel and, with the help of fellow workers from England, made many converts in Thuringia, Hesse, Franconia, and Bavaria. Among the monasteries he founded to support the new faith was the great Benedictine center of learning and priestly education at Fulda. Consecrated archbishop of Mainz c. 746, Boniface, as primate of Germany, organized the church and provided for its discipline during a period of confusion and disorder. In old age he returned to the scene of his early mission in Friesland and there witnessed to his faith in martyrdom at the hands of pagan worshipers of Wotan.

Some of the ablest men and women of the Middle Ages entered monasteries. Here their prayers and worship kept faith alive; their hands ministered to the poor, the sick, and the hungry; their keen minds served the cause of scholarship and education; and their belief in an orderly world ruled by a God who is trustworthy and unfailing helped to lay the foundations on which rational science could develop. In a period of political disorder and ceaseless, grinding toil, only in the monasteries could scholars find the safe retreat and necessary leisure in which to study and write. In these more or less inviolate havens scribes copied the Scriptures and other holy books, and artists created exquisite illuminations, paintings, architecture, sculpture, music, embroidery, metal-work, and glass-work—all in the service of Christianity and to the glory of God.

The effectiveness and popularity of the monasteries brought them wealth and power. This in turn attracted the indolent and those who wished merely to escape from the dangers and cares of the world. When monastic discipline became lax and spiritual zeal declined, a series of reform movements appeared.

In 910 William the Pius, duke of Aquitaine, founded a monastery at Cluny that grew to be the chief religious and cultural center of Europe during the 10th and 11th centuries. The reforms instituted under its first two abbots, Berno and Odo, were widely imitated in the nearly one thousand communities under its jurisdiction. As a result of the Cluny movement, new churches were built, the liturgy was developed, many schools were established, and the scriptoria were enlarged.

The austere Cistercian Order was founded in 1098 in the forest wilderness at Citeaux near Dijon in protest against what had become the luxury and architectural extravagance of the Cluniac Order. The Cistercians dominated monasticism in the 12th century. Their third abbot, the English monastic reformer Stephen Harding (d. 1134), organized the arduous, self-denying life of the order. His monks spent less time in worship than in the heavy labor of clearing the land, draining the swamps, and thus creating rich farmland. The Cistercians introduced wool culture into England and better farming techniques into Europe, both of great economic significance. In a century and a half more than six hundred monasteries became affiliated with Citeaux under the authority of its abbot.

The best known of the Cistercians is the prominent medieval saint Bernard (1090-1153), founder of the monastery of Clairvaux and for many years its abbot. His interest in music prompted him to write in one of his letters that church music should "radiate" Christian truth and please the ear in order to move the heart. By achieving a golden mean between the frivolous and the harsh, it should affect man's nature. His writings and sermons, reflecting as they do the words, style, and thoughts of the Scriptures, show his thorough knowledge of the Holy Books. He encouraged a revival of Bible study but declared that it was more important to move men's hearts than expound the Scriptures. At the height of his fame as the greatest preacher of his age and the most powerful religious leader in western Europe, he issued the call to the ill-fated Second Crusade.

With the revival of town life in the 13th century a new type of Christian service was required. Until now the church had ministered primarily to a rural population, but in this period there arose various orders of mendicant friars whose vocation was to meet the needs of the townsfolk. The monk, as his name indicates (Greek *monachos*, "solitary"), was a person apart, but the friar (Latin *frater*, "brother"; Middle English *frier*, "brother") broke away from the monastic enclosure to preach and teach wherever people lived.

The Order of Black Friars, or the Dominican Order, was established by the Castilian churchman Dominic (1170-1221), who, with his band of poor preachers, became a successful missionary in Languedoc. Active both in preaching and study, the Dominicans taught in the newly founded universities. Eventually their beggar's bag of mendicant days was transformed into the present academic "hood."

The founder of the Grey Friars, or the Franciscan Order, was the beloved and certainly the best-known saint of the Middle Ages, Francis of Assisi (1182-1226). With his gaiety, simplicity, and singleness of purpose and with his respect for all living creatures as his brothers and sisters, he embodied the highest spiritual ideals of the period. The inspiration for founding his order of Barefoot Friars came to Francis one morning at Mass when the priest read how Jesus sent forth the Twelve to preach the gospel (Matthew 10.5-14). His order attracted the finest minds and noblest spirits of the age and eventually produced four popes and many scholars.

As will be noted below, these two mendicant orders, through their outstanding scholars, made significant contributions to scholasticism and to the growth of the universities.

Chapter 18 Christian Learning—Scholasticism

Scholasticism originated in the early monastery and cathedral schools in which intellectual activity began to awaken after centuries of stagnation. It was the medieval system of Christian thought based on the authority of the Bible, the Church Fathers, and Aristotle. The beginning of scholasticism is usually traced to Anselm, the abbot of the monastery of Bec who became archbishop of Canterbury in 1093. He propounded the famous ontological proof of the existence of God, asserting that because our minds can conceive of the idea of a perfect, ultimate being, God must therefore exist in reality. Anselm's motto, *fides quaerens intelligentiam*, "faith seeking understanding," stands for the conviction of the schoolmen that the understanding gained through reason and logic can reinforce and illuminate faith and the doctrines of the church.

Medieval philosophers believed that faith and reason formed two parts of a great whole, and they were confident that human minds could bring these two into harmony. In an age of superstition and of a piety that was often irrational the scholastics attempted to establish the reasonable basis of Christianity. Their disputations, it is true, sometimes descended to hairsplitting distinctions. They asked such questions as how many angels can stand on the point of a needle. Nevertheless, their quest for a reasonable faith aroused zeal for learning and made precise thought and clear expression necessary. As a result, crowds of students flocked to the new universities, especially to Paris and Oxford, both famous for their teachers of philosophy and theology. At this time the Bible became one of the chief subjects of academic study. The University of Paris, founded in the 12th century, was a leading center for the study of Aristotle, whose philosophy was introduced into the West between 1120 and 1220, largely through the writings both of the Spanish-Arabian philosopher Averroës and the Hebrew scholar Maimonides. Among the teachers who attracted students from all parts of Europe to the great centers of learning in the 12th century were Peter Abelard, William of Champeaux, Hugh of St. Victor, and Peter Lombard.

In the 13th century, scholasticism attained its highest development under the Dominican and Franciscan scholars of Paris and Oxford. The two outstanding Dominicans in this movement were: Albertus Magnus (d. 1280), one of the earliest scholars of Aristotelian thought; and his pupil Thomas Aquinas (d. 1274), who, it is said, "Christianized Aristotle." Aquinas, a towering intellectual figure of the Middle Ages, began his *Summa Theologiae* in 1265 in order to reconcile reason with religion. Deeply influenced by this epoch-making work, Dante, the supreme medieval poet, created an imaginative expression of Aquinas's philosophy and theology in his *Divine Comedy*. Today, Thomas Aquinas's *Summa* is the basis of Roman Catholic theological instruction. His system of theology is referred to as Thomism.

The Franciscans tended to oppose Thomism. Bonaventura (d. 1274), the biographer of St. Francis and the administrator of the Franciscan order, disagreed with Thomas Aquinas, his friend and colleague at the University of Paris. His controversy with Aquinas originated in his fear that too much reason might destroy faith. He accepted the teachings of Aristotle only so far as they were compatible with Christian revelation and tradition.

The Oxford Franciscans carried the opposition to Aquinas even further. One of them, Roger Bacon (d. 1294), a schoolman far ahead of his time in natural science, criticized scholars who relied on Aristotle for all knowledge. Rather than concentrating on poor Latin versions of Aristotle (Bacon himself knew Greek and Hebrew), he urged scholars to experiment with real things, for he believed that, in time, by discovering the principles governing real things people would be able to fly, ride in horseless carriages, and travel in ships without oars or sails.

Duns Scotus (d. 1308) belonged to the Franciscans of Oxford and was the ablest logical thinker among the scholastics. In the new and influential theological system Duns Scotus developed, he taught that, though much in theology leaves room for philosophical doubt, it must, nevertheless, be accepted on the authority of the church. At this point the elaborate intellectual structure of scholasticism began to crack.

Finally, William of Ockham (d. 1349), a pupil of Duns Scotus and, like his master, a Franciscan teacher at Oxford, declared that the truths revealed by faith were beyond the range of reason and that Christian theology could not be forced into the alien form of Aristotelianism. This sounded the knell for scholasticism. Ockham taught that true authority for the Christian rests not on the decisions of popes and councils but in the Bible alone—a teaching that earned for this 14th-century Franciscan scholar Martin Luther's accolade of "dear master."

Though scholasticism failed to explain in a rational manner all church doctrines, it created a structure of medieval thought as bold, intricate, rich, and subtle as the Gothic architecture that originated in the Middle Ages. Moreover, its failure in its primary task does not obscure the ultimate success of scholasticism in teaching people how to think and in delivering Europe from its long night of intellectual darkness.

Chapter 19 The Papacy

The papacy developed into one of the outstanding institutions of the Middle Ages. Originally all bishops and priests were called "pope," from the Latin *papa*, "father," but as early as the 6th century the name was used as the special title of the bishop of Rome. Not until the 9th century, however, did Gregory VII specifically rule that only the bishop of Rome should be called "pope."

The pre-eminence of the church of Rome was based, first, on the tradition that the apostle Peter had founded it and had been its first bishop, and, second, on three Gospel passages (Matthew 16.18-19; Luke 22.32; John 21.15-17) that were interpreted as implying Peter's divinely ordained leadership of the entire church.

As early as the 5th century, Leo the Great (c. 400-461), the bishop who saved Rome from Attila the Hun, declared that Peter's primacy among the apostles, in both faith and government, belonged to Peter's successors, the bishops of Rome. In 445 he procured from Emperor Valentinian III an edict commanding all bishops and clergy to obey the bishop of Rome because he held "the primacy of Peter."

The growing importance of the papacy was strengthened by Gregory the Great (c. 540-604), the first of sixteen popes of that name. His talent for administration and his Roman devotion to an ordered society and the rule of law contributed to the success of his spiritual leadership. He was born into a wealthy senatorial family, and when he became a monk, he established seven Benedictine monasteries on his family estates. One day, according to the well-known story, Gregory saw some fair-haired slave-boys being offered for sale in the Roman Forum. "Who are they?" he asked. On being told they were Angles from Britain, he declared, "Not Angles, they have the faces of angels and should be heirs with the angels in heaven." So keen was his desire to convert the British that he himself set out on a mission to them, but after a three-day journey he was recalled by the pope.

Elected pope himself by acclamation in 590, he accepted the office despite chronic illness. He was the first monk to become pope. Occupying this high office during the declining power of civil authority, he raised armies against the Lombards, issued orders to generals, appointed governors of cities, repaired aqueducts, fed the poor from the estates of the church, and communicated with the kings of Europe. These actions established precedents for the temporal power of the papacy. As pope he maintained strict discipline among the clergy. He also insisted on the primacy of the papacy against the ecumenical claims of the patriarch of Constantinople. In 596, still determined to evangelize Britain, Gregory sent his friend, later to be known as Augustine of Canterbury, with forty monks from his own monastery in Rome to carry the gospel to the Anglo-Saxons. The missionaries landed in Kent, established their base in Canterbury, and began the slow conversion of England.

Gregory was in many ways the most remarkable of the early medieval popes. According to Williston Walker's *A History of the Christian Church*, "In him the Western Church of the Middle Ages already exhibited its characteristic traits, whether of doctrine, life, worship, or organization. Its growth was to be in the directions in which Gregory had moved." He called himself *Servus Servorum Dei*, "Servant of the Servants of God"; his abilities as a preacher and scholar, however, made him an outstanding leader. As a writer he spread the doctrines of the great Augustine, bishop of Hippo. At a period when liturgical music had grown so diversified in the widely scattered churches that the unity of worship and even of faith was threatened, Gregory helped to develop a single type of Christian music for the Mass. This music, called the Gregorian chant, or plainsong, is a modal style between singing and speaking.

Conflicts arising from the relations between the papacy and secular rulers dominated the Middle Ages. Pepin the Short, son of Charles Martel and father of Charlemagne, desired church sanction before he deposed the last powerless king of the Merovingian dynasty and assumed for himself the kingship of the Franks. Accordingly, he appealed to Pope Zacharias. He promptly approved Pepin's request, declaring, "It is better that he who has the power in the state should be called king, rather than he who is falsely called king." In the old Germanic ceremony of kingship, Pepin had himself raised aloft on the shields of his Frankish nobles, but was anointed and crowned by the religious authorities in 751, thereafter assuming the title *Gratia Dei Rex Francorum*, "King of the Franks by the Grace of God." Thus a new idea of kingship arose when, in the words of the English historian Edward Gibbon, "A German chieftain was transformed into the Lord's anointed." A king "by the grace of God" would now be regarded as God's representative on earth. Thus his subjects' obedience to him could henceforth be considered their religious duty.

On the other hand, Pepin's anointing and crowning with the consent of the pope established the principle of the pope's power to give or to withhold kingdoms, a principle underlying many disputes between the popes and the secular rulers of the Middle Ages.

The next pope, Stephen II, enhanced the prestige of Pepin's new title by traveling to the church of St. Denis near Paris and there recrowning Pepin. He also anointed Pepin and his sons, conferring on them the somewhat vague title, "Patricians of the Romans." In return for the pope's endorsement Pepin invaded Italy and defeated the Lombards. In recognition of the claim of the popes to be heirs of the empire in Italy, Pepin presented the pope with the conquered territory of Ravenna, which had formerly belonged to the Byzantine Empire. This so-called Donation of Pepin of 756 had long-lasting consequences: it laid the foundations for the Papal States and initiated the temporal power of the papacy, a power that survived until 1870.

Pepin's son, Charles the Great, better known as Charlemagne (742-814), more than doubled his father's realm and, by his recreation of an empire, established the idea of the Holy Roman Empire. A truly remarkable person— being a warrior, administrator, patron of learning and education, as well as a devoted son of the church—Charlemagne was one of the most admired rulers of the Middle Ages. Like his father, Charlemagne was crowned by the pope. When Leo III placed the imperial Roman crown on his head as he knelt in St. Peter's church in Rome on Christmas Day 800, the idea of church and state being two closely related aspects of the kingdom of God seemed to have become an actuality. Inspired by his study of Augustine's *City of God*, Charlemagne believed himself to be the earthly head of the empire under God. In a letter to Leo, Charlemagne compared the pope to Aaron and himself to Moses. Charlemagne's aim was to work with the pope and support him, but not to obey him.

In the struggle that raged between church and state during the 11th century, great princes tried to control the church and its vast estates, while popes claimed supremacy over rulers. At a low point in the church's history, when corruption was widespread and the papacy itself cynically bought and sold, there appeared the strongest and most noteworthy of the medieval popes. He was Hildebrand, who was born in Tuscany and educated in Rome in a Cluniac monastery. In 1073, during the funeral of Pope

Alexander II in St. John Lateran, the crowd, despite the fact that Hildebrand had twice refused the papacy, acclaimed him as pope and carried him to the church of St. Peter-in-Chains where they enthroned him.

Hildebrand took the name of Gregory VII (c. 1020-1085) and immediately initiated reforms to free the church from secular domination so as to make the papacy supreme. In this endeavor he was apparently free from personal ambition and single-mindedly devoted to his spiritual responsibility of shepherding his Christian flock during a period of lawlessness and even savagery. He believed that a pope's power was a divine gift given only for the purpose of saving souls and transforming human institutions according to Christian principles. From clergy, laity, and rulers alike he demanded absolute obedience to papal orders. He warned the kings of France, England, and Germany to forsake their evil ways and obey his counsels. He explained to William the Conqueror that the pope's power is superior to that of the king because the pope is responsible at the Last Day for the king. Gregory excommunicated the German emperor, Henry IV, for opposing him. Henry, to obtain release from this sentence, came to the pope (then staying at Canossa) and abased himself as a barefoot penitent in the snow. This scene represents the deepest humiliation of medieval temporal power before the power of the church.

In the 13th century Innocent III (1198-1216), a medieval pope renowned for his ability, learning, and statecraft, raised the temporal power of the papacy to its greatest height. He believed that since things of the spirit are superior to things of the body, and since the church rules the spirit and earthly monarchs rule the body, then earthly monarchs must be subject to the pope. Acting on his theory of papal supremacy, he claimed and exercised authority over the kingdoms of Europe,

> "to pluck up and break down,
> to destroy and to overthrow,
> to build and to plant."
>
> Jeremiah 1.10

Among his political acts he dictated the choice of the ruler of the Holy Roman Empire and crowned Otto of Brunswick as emperor. Because Otto broke his promises to the pope, Innocent III excommunicated him and chose Frederick II as his successor.

When, contrary to King John's wishes, Innocent III chose Stephen Langton to be archbishop of Canterbury, John persecuted the English clergy and seized church lands. Innocent III retaliated by putting England under an interdict, so that for six years church bells were silent and church doors closed against the faithful. Finally, the pope excommunicated John and induced the French to plan an invasion of England. Insecure at home, the king in 1213 submitted to the pope as his feudal lord and agreed to pay him a large annual tax. Alarmed by the possibilities stemming from this new alliance of the pope and the king, the English barons led by Archbishop Stephen Langton put a curb on the arbitrary despotism of the king by forcing him, at Runnymede, to acknowledge their rights as stated in the Magna Charta—a document denounced by the pope.

To crown his pontificate, Innocent III convened the brilliant Fourth Lateran Council of 1215, which passed laws defining the pope's ideas for the church and firmly establishing a concept of papal supremacy which would endure for the remainder of the century.

Although papal secular power reached its zenith in the 13th century, it began to decline rather rapidly thereafter. From 1309 to 1377 the French kings virtually controlled the papacy during the so-called Babylonian Captivity when all the popes were French and lived at Avignon on the river Rhône. Owing largely to the persuasions of two saintly women, Catherine of Siena and Bridget of Sweden, the papacy recovered from its degradation and moved back to Rome. Immediately, however, the papal schism ensued, lasting from 1378 to 1417, when two and sometimes three rival popes claimed the papal throne. The Council of Constance endeavored to end this schism by transforming the papacy from an absolute to a constitutional sovereignty, but their efforts largely failed. Although the papal court of the 15th century patronized the greatest artists of the West and made Rome a brilliant Renaissance capital, the papacy, spiritually, had reached so low a level under popes like Alexander VI that reaction set in leading to the Protestant Reformation.

Chapter 20 **The Crusades**

Jerusalem, which had been the goal of countless pilgrims even before Constantine built the Church of the Holy Sepulcher in the 4th century, became increasingly important in the Middle Ages because Christians placed a great value on both relics and pilgrimages. Even after the Moslems captured Jerusalem from the Byzantine Empire in 638, pilgrimages to the Holy Land continued unhindered because the Arabs shared the veneration of Christians for places associated with the life of Christ. However, when the Seljuk Turks took Jerusalem in the 11th century, they harassed Christian pilgrims and desecrated the Church of the Holy Sepulcher. These provocations were one of the causes of the Crusades.

In 1095 Urban II (c. 1042-1099), an eloquent and learned pope and a friend of Gregory VII, received an appeal from the Byzantine emperor Alexis. The Seljuk Turks were threatening Constantinople and Alexis asked for the pope's help. That year Urban proclaimed the First Crusade in a fervent and extremely successful address delivered at the Synod of Clermont in eastern France. He called upon all Christians to aid the hard-pressed Emperor Alexis and also to deliver the Holy Places from Moslem control. The pope appealed to knights and soldiers to cease their killing of Christian brothers in order to help their fellow Christians in the East. "Enter upon the road to the Holy Sepulcher; wrest the land from the wicked infidels and subject it to yourselves," he exhorted them. The whole assembly, fired with enthusiasm, exclaimed with one accord, "It is the will of God." With this as a rallying cry, the First Crusade began.

The initial enthusiasm was fanned by Peter the Hermit, a monk from Amiens, who, through his inspiring preaching, communicated his intense concern for the Holy Land to people of all kinds, from peasants to kings. Those who enlisted in the First Crusade did so from a variety of motives. Some hoped for adventure, honor, or spoils. Others set out with deep religious feelings, believing that they were acting for Christ and for the sake of their own souls. They wore a cross on their chests as they went forth and on their backs when they returned.

Three great armies raised by the nobility of Europe set out for the East in August 1096, but Jerusalem was not captured until July 1099. After slaughtering the city's Moslem inhabitants, the crusaders established a feudal regime, the Kingdom of Jerusalem. Godfrey of Bouillon, the duke of Lorraine, ruled Jerusalem with the title of Defender of the Holy Sepulcher, but after his death in 1100 his brother succeeded him as King Baldwin I (1100-1118).

The Holy Land was divided into four archbishoprics and ten bishoprics all under a Latin patriarch living in Jerusalem. Many monasteries were established. Italian merchants, who had supplied the armies, settled in the larger towns. Several religious orders of soldier-monks, of which the Knights Templars and the Knights Hospitalers were the most important, provided the main defense of the crusaders' kingdom.

The Second Crusade, promoted by no less a person than Bernard, abbot of Clairvaux, ended in failure. News that Jerusalem and most of the Holy Land had been lost to the Moslems in 1187 induced Emperor Frederick Barbarossa, King Philip Augustus of France, and King Richard the Lion-Hearted of England to organize the Third Crusade. After the Emperor was accidentally drowned, the two other allies quarreled, causing the expedition to fail. During the Fourth Crusade, Constantinople was captured at the earnest request of the Venetians who furnished the transportation. Ironically, at this time the great church of Hagia Sophia was plundered by Christian warriors. The Children's Crusade of 1212 was a pathetically misguided episode. Other Crusades followed, the Ninth and last being that of 1271 led by Prince Edward of England, later Edward I.

Despite the huge cost in lives and treasure during nearly two hundred years, the Crusades failed in their stated objective. Jerusalem was lost in 1244. Acre, the last Christian stronghold, fell in 1291, ending the Christian control of the Holy Land. The indirect effects of the Crusades, however, were incalculable. They stimulated commerce, opened trade routes down the Rhine and across the Alps, and brought great wealth to the merchants of Genoa, Venice, Pisa, and other cities. The need to raise money with which to supply the crusaders caused the break-up of feudal holdings. This eventually led to the growth of towns and the formation of craftsmen's and merchants' guilds. More importantly, the Crusades provided a liberal education and a less provincial outlook to many who had never before ventured beyond their own village or castle. From the ancient civilizations of the East the crusaders brought back reports of luxurious living, handsome buildings, splendid cities, and all the distinctive art and culture of the East. Moreover, contact with highly intelligent people like the Arabs stimulated dormant minds.

Europe soon experienced an intellectual awakening fostered by the continuing pilgrimages to such shrines as those in Jerusalem, Rome, Compostella in Spain, and Canterbury in England. As has already been noted, religious movements arose, universities were founded under church auspices, the theology and philosophy of the Middle Ages known as Scholasticism flourished, Gothic cathedrals were built, and a vernacular literature appeared in the works of writers like Chaucer. As the Middle Ages reached their final flowering, the Oxford scholar, John Wycliffe, made the entire Bible available in the English language.

Chapter 21 **The Bible**

In the 6th century, at the beginning of the Middle Ages, Pope Gregory the Great insisted that the Bible is the essential source of all religious learning. He believed it to be inspired and to possess an inner spiritual meaning, but he counseled readers to study its obvious, historical meaning before seeking its hidden message. To understand the Bible, he said, people must love it and follow its teachings. "We hear the words of God," he wrote, "if we act upon them." Again he wrote, "Throughout the Scriptures, God speaks to us for this purpose alone, to lead us to the love of himself and of our neighbor."

With the coming of the long night of barbarism and the end of Greco-Roman civilization in the West, the Bible-reading that had deepened and nourished the lives of Christians, and provided intellectual stimulus for their leaders during the first five Christian centuries, declined and almost ceased. Many lay people, now listening to the Latin Scriptures read to them in church, found them almost unintelligible, for Latin was no longer the spoken language. Children were not taught to read and illiteracy reigned in Christian households and even among many of the clergy. Books had become scarce and very costly. A copy of the Bible might be as expensive to buy as a house. In this chaotic and ignorant period preachers could no longer expect, as John Chrysostom once did, that their congregations would come to church having already studied the Sunday lesson.

During the darkest period, however, a few Christians cherished the Bible. In remote monasteries patient hands copied it. Eager eyes studied it. Monks and nuns used it in their devotions and lived by its precepts. Especially in the Irish monasteries, with their emphasis on scholarship and evangelism, the Scriptures were preserved, transcribed, studied, and carried far and wide as the basis of missionary preaching and the guide to Christian life.

Charlemagne, convinced of the value of classical and Biblical learning, invited the eminent British churchman and scholar, Alcuin of York, to establish the Palace School at Aachen as a school for the sons of the nobility and a college for the royal family, the clergy, and the court. Alcuin (735-804) had been educated at the cathedral school of York by a disciple of the Anglo-Saxon churchman and scholar, the Venerable Bede, and had thus received as fine an education as any then available in Western Europe. When he accepted Charlemagne's invitation, he brought to the Continent the learning that had taken refuge and had developed in the British Isles during the barbarian invasions. Charlemagne himself attended the Palace School and learned to read, but he never mastered the skill of writing. At Aachen, Alcuin established the medieval study of the seven liberal arts: the trivium (grammar, rhetoric, logic), and the quadrivium (arithmetic, geometry, astronomy, music). He is also credited with revising the text of the Vulgate, whose spelling, punctuation, and grammar had become corrupt in the hands of careless copyists. A copy of the Gospels revised by Alcuin was presented to Charlemagne in 800 at his coronation in Rome.

Like Charlemagne before him, Alfred the Great (871-900), king of the West Saxons, encouraged learning by inviting a group of eminent scholars to establish a court school for youths, clergy, and nobles. Though most of his life was spent battling the Danes, he strengthened the English church by restoring learning among the clergy and promoting the reading of the Bible. Though no sure proof of it exists, some scholars think that Alfred translated the first fifty psalms into Anglo-Saxon.

As knowledge of the Bible increased little by little, its teachings exercised a greater influence on the basic values of society. To help those who knew little Latin, vernacular glosses, or explanations, were often inserted between the lines of Scripture. From the 12th century on, the Bible became the subject of academic study in the cathedral schools and universities under such masters as Anselm, Peter Lombard, Abelard, and Hugh of St. Victor. Commentaries on the text were written. Treatises in question and answer form were produced. Even before printing from moveable type was invented, pilgrims and monks traveled with small, illustrated Gospel block books in their pockets. The pictures in these were stamped from wood blocks and the text usually written by hand. These "Bibles of the Poor" not only spread the Bible message but also influenced the development of Christian iconography.

Until the end of the Middle Ages the Bible spoke to the mass of the people chiefly through the liturgy, which was largely a collection and arrangement of Biblical texts. These were set in such an order that they provided forms of public worship having profound and inexhaustible meaning. The Psalms were prominent in church services and appealed to medieval people because the words of these ancient songs and poems seemed to voice their own prayers.

During the Mass special honor was paid to the Gospel book as the symbol of Christ himself. A deacon, accompanied by two torch bearers and a sub-deacon with a thurible, carried the book from the altar to the reading desk while the people removed their headgear, put aside swords and canes, and stood to hear the Gospel lesson read. Many surviving Gospel books are written in beautiful scripts and are often adorned with illuminations depicting

Biblical scenes. The care and artistry lavished on these books attest to the living faith of those who commissioned them, made them, and used them. Given by kings and nobles to each other, or to monasteries and cathedrals, the most sumptuous of these volumes are bound between gold covers and decorated by skillful medieval goldsmiths. Some of these covers are adorned with carved ivory panels or studded with jewels.

Before the new age dawned, it was evident that the Bible had become the basic book of the Middle Ages. It trained men and women in the things of the spirit, and its words, ideas, and stories filled their minds. The Latin of Jerome's Vulgate was eventually transformed into the medieval Latin of educated people, and later it influenced the various vernacular languages that arose among the masses. The Bible was used as the textbook of elementary education. It promoted learning and research in the newly founded universities. It enriched literature and religious drama. It initiated reform within the church. In short, it was one of the chief factors in the creation of the new age.

The Bible furnished medieval artists and craftsmen with an almost infinite array of subjects to depict in sculptured stone or colored glass, in manuscript illuminations, in tapestry, embroidery, metal work, carved wood or ivory, enamel, ceramics, and fresco painting. These workers in many mediums believed that their skills were the gift of God, as of old it had been with Bezalel, of whom Moses said that he was filled "with the Spirit of God, with ability, with intelligence, with knowledge, and with all craftsmanship, to devise artistic designs, to work in gold and silver and bronze, in cutting stones for setting, and in carving wood, for work in every skilled craft" (Exodus 35.31-33). Their designs, whether for a cathedral or for the initial letter of a manuscript, aimed to reveal the beauty that the Middle Ages believed to be the *splendor veritatis*, the radiance of truth.

The Bible

Biblical ideas and images inspired much in Gothic architecture. In the great churches, abbeys, and cathedrals that are its glory, this architecture still gives visible expression to the faith and spiritual vitality of the Middle Ages. People then believed that the ultimate reality in which they lived and moved and had their being was the unseen spiritual world—a realm of divine beauty and harmony. To symbolize this invisible harmony of God's entire creation, medieval stone masons and architects worked to achieve perfect order and proportion in all parts of their buildings. Their cathedrals, many of which still dominate their surroundings as Christianity dominated the lives of medieval men and women, impressed those who saw them with the idea that here was the very abode of God and the center of his kingdom on earth.

"Awesome is this place," chanted those who, in the brilliance of light and color and royal splendor, dedicated the new choir of Canterbury Cathedral in 1130. "Truly, this is the house of God and the gate of heaven, and it will be called the court of the Lord." According to the account of this occasion in *Annales Monastici,* Henry I, who was present at the dedication with all the great men of England, "swore with his royal oath . . . that truly [the sanctuary] was awesome."

Abbot Suger's rebuilding, in 1144, of the facade, narthex, and choir of the abbey church of St. Denis near Paris signaled the emergence of the new Gothic style. It featured pointed arches, flying buttresses, and rib vaults, all used in a harmonious design to enliven the downward thrust of heavy masonry and to convey, by means of light and line, the living splendor of the Heavenly City in which God dwells with man. To reinforce the impression produced on the beholder by a Gothic cathedral in all its radiance of colored glass, the Epistle read at its dedication began, "And I saw the holy city, new Jerusalem, coming down out of heaven from God . . ." (Revelation 21.2-5). In describing the light-filled choir of St. Denis with its twelve supporting columns, Suger quoted a passage from Ephesians to express the symbolism of the design: "You are built upon the foundation laid by the apostles and prophets, and Christ Jesus himself is the foundation-stone [or the keystone]. In him the whole building is bonded together and grows into a holy temple in the Lord" (Ephesians 2.20-22, NEB). With this Biblical image in mind, medieval builders and sculptors frequently carved a representation or symbol of Christ on the ornamented keystones, or bosses, of Gothic vaults. In fact the whole structure with all its images and ornaments, its light and lines and colors, served as a summary of medieval religious thought, becoming a veritable Bible of the people.

The Bible itself, once the possession of only the wealthy and the educated, made its first, abbreviated appearance among unlettered people, as we have noted, during the 14th and 15th centuries in popular illustrated Bibles called *Biblia Pauperium*. Most of these were really picture books with explanatory texts in the vernacular.

The idea of making the entire Bible available to everyone in the newly emerging English language seems to have originated with John Wycliffe (c. 1320-1384), master of Balliol College at Oxford, statesman, religious reformer, and the father of English prose. His studies and his political experience convinced him that the only valid authority in spiritual matters was neither the pope, nor the clergy, nor church tradition, but solely the Bible. At that time very few lay people, or even ordinary priests, could understand the meaning of the sonorous Latin of Jerome's Vulgate, which was the only version available to them. Nevertheless, Wycliffe was confident that if everyone, people and clergy alike, read and studied the Bible, it would end the corruption that had crept into religious institutions, purify the life of the church, and renew Christianity.

Accordingly, Wycliffe gathered a group of scholars who made an English translation of the Vulgate in 1382. Because printing had not yet been introduced, Wycliffe's first and subsequent versions were handwritten volumes that had to be painstakingly and expensively copied. To overcome this difficulty, Wycliffe organized his "poor priests"—his itinerant Lollards, who, barefooted, dressed in long robes, and carrying a staff, wandered two by two throughout England, preaching his doctrines and bringing knowledge of his Bible to the people. Despite vigorous opposition from the authorities of both church and state, all of whom saw this movement for what it was, a challenge to their power, the Lollards quietly continued their work until the beginning of the Reformation.

With Wycliffe, the Middle Ages began to draw to a close. Opposition to his ideas, however, was so severe that his revolution changed little in England. Inspired by Wycliffe's doctrines, Bohemian students at Oxford, including the martyr Jerome of Prague, returned home to broadcast them in the University of Prague. Their message encouraged the religious reformer, John Huss, to continue to protest against church corruption and to exalt the Bible as the "law of God." These actions finally resulted in his own martyrdom.

Part Five
The Eastern Orthodox Churches 1054-1980

Chapter 22 East and West in Conflict

While the Middle Ages were running their course in Western Europe, a different development was taking place in the East. Within the theoretically unified church of the early centuries, the Fourth Ecumenical Council of Chalcedon of 451 had recognized five jurisdictions. Each was headed by a patriarch, who was a bishop having authority over other bishops. The five patriarchates were: Rome, Constantinople, Alexandria, Antioch, and Jerusalem. Furthermore, the Council of Chalcedon decreed that the patriarch of Constantinople was the single head of the entire Eastern Church. This office placed him in practical equality with the bishop of Rome. When Leo I, who was then bishop of Rome, vigorously opposed the decree, his opposition foreshadowed the ultimate separation of the churches of the East from those of the West.

The Great Schism of 1054, which neither East nor West desired, was the result of the two sides moving farther apart in many areas. Besides language, there were cultural, political, and religious differences separating the eastern and western churches. In the 3rd century Latin had supplanted Greek in the West, but Greek continued to be the Christian language of the East. The barbarian invasions of the early

Middle Ages greatly diminished the cultural life of the West, while in the East it continued to flourish. In the West the pope was often more powerful than the government, but in the East the church remained under the imperial control that Constantine had established. During the iconoclastic controversy of the 8th and 9th centuries, in the East Emperor Leo III forbade the use of images in worship and enforced his decree through the use of his army. In the West the pope and the people resisted him. East and West soon ceased to be in communion with each other. Finally, the Great Schism of 1054 divided Christendom into the Eastern Orthodox Church and the Western Roman Catholic Church. The chief issue separating these two Christian bodies was, and still remains, the rejection by the East of the jurisdiction of the pope.

Chapter 23 The Eastern Empire and the Church

During the chaotic and difficult years of the Middle Ages in the West, Constantinople remained the chief repository of Greek and Roman culture and the center of the most advanced and sophisticated civilization in the world. The city, surrounded by a triple wall of fortifications that made it virtually impregnable, became the largest and wealthiest in Europe. Its parks and paved streets, its imperial palaces and other buildings all filled with artistic and literary treasures, and its churches, especially Hagia Sophia, excited the wonder and admiration of travelers from many lands, including Britons, Jews, Arabs, Goths, and Norsemen. Russian envoys from Kiev in the 10th century, describing their awestruck impression of the church of Hagia Sophia, wrote, "We only know that God dwells there among men and their service is fairer than the ceremonies of other nations; for we cannot forget that beauty."

The Emperor Justinian (527-565) had succeeded in dominating the Eastern church to a greater degree than any previous emperor, making it virtually a department of the state. Regarded as Christ's representative on earth, the emperor became the church's guardian and the convener of its ecumenical councils. But political domination, misunderstandings, jealousies, and sincere differences of opinion about the Person of Christ had kept the four eastern patriarchates in almost continual conflict, thus weakening the church.

Chapter 24 **Gains and Losses in the East**

A bitter theological controversy about the exact definition of the Person of Christ centered around Nestorius, a Syrian churchman famous for his asceticism and eloquence. He became patriarch of Constantinople in 428 at a time when pious people expressed their reverence for Mary the mother of Jesus by calling her, "Mother of God." Nestorius preached against the use of this title believing that it tended to obscure the distinction between Christ's human and his divine nature. Cyril, patriarch of Alexandria, seeing in this teaching an opportunity to humiliate a rival patriarch, accused Nestorius of trying to split the personality of Christ. Nestorius, however, had declared, "With the one name Christ we designate at the same time two natures." Nevertheless, jealousy, ambition, and partisanship so exaggerated whatever subtle differences separated the doctrines of Nestorius and Cyril that the dispute eventually involved the emperors of both East and West. In the end it destroyed the unity of Christendom. The Council of Ephesus of 431 condemned and deposed Nestorius without a hearing. He withdrew to his old monastery at Antioch, but was later banished by the emperor to Arabia. Afterwards the imperial Eastern Church persecuted the followers of Nestorius, causing their Syrian leader to flee to Persia. There he established vigorous new Nestorian churches.

Such great zeal for evangelism developed in the Nestorian churches that in the 6th century they sent missionaries to the Malabar coast of India. There they founded or re-established the Mar Thoma Church, the oldest native Christian community existing in India today.

In the 7th century Nestorian Christians, after penetrating to central China, converted a few followers in Shensi Province. In Sian, the center of Nestorian missionary activity, a curious stone monument erected in 781 still commemorates the founding of the church and states in Chinese and Syriac that the New Testament contains twenty-seven books. After this first Chinese Christian community perished, the Nestorian missionaries persisted, again reaching China in the 13th century and converting many among the Tartar and Turkish tribes. A Turkish princess of the Nestorian faith was the mother of Kublai Khan, the Mongol ruler of a vast Chinese empire. His court at Peiping was visited by the Venetian traveler, Marco Polo. Nestorian Christians were protected by Kublai Khan and an archbishopric was established at the capital in 1275.

In reaction to Nestorian beliefs, there developed in the Eastern Church during the 5th and 6th centuries a doctrine called Monophysitism from a Greek word meaning "one nature." Though this doctrine declared that Christ has only one nature in which the human and divine are indistinguishable, its result was to emphasize the divine. Monophysitism was condemned by the Orthodox Church but embraced by various churches in the East. The Egyptians accepted Monophysitism, probably less from theological conviction than from their resentment of Greek domination of the Orthodox Church. They established their own independent national Coptic Church which survives today, as does its daughter Ethiopian Church. The Ethiopian Church was originally founded in the middle of the 4th century by Frumentius who had been consecrated bishop of Axum by Athanasius of Alexandria. Palestine, Syria, and Armenia followed the example of Egypt in establishing independent, national churches. The Syrian Monophysite Church (the Jacobite Church of

Syria) exists today in the Tigris Valley and has adherents in South India.

These theological controversies so eroded the Eastern Orthodox Church that when fanatical Moslem armies invaded Christian lands in the 7th century, the empire could not prevent the Mohammedans from taking Syria, Palestine, Egypt, all of North Africa, and Sicily in the name of Allah. They established a Moslem state as far west as Spain. Mohammed's followers were finally expelled from France in the decisive battle of Tours in 732 by Charles Martel, grandfather of Charlemagne.

The Eastern Church partly offset its losses to Islam by expanding northward into the Slavic principalities of the Balkans and Russia. At the invitation of the duke of Moravia the eastern emperor sent two high officials, the brothers Cyril and Methodius, as missionaries to the Slavs in 864. In preparation for their mission Cyril is reputed to have invented the Slavic script called Cyrillic, which became the foundation of the Russian alphabet. Methodius spent his last years translating the Bible into Slavic.

Czar Boris of Bulgaria, after his baptism in 864 and the introduction of Christianity to his kingdom, acknowledged the spiritual leadership of Constantinople, while the patriarch recognized the Bulgarian Church as a self-governing body. In the 12th century the Serbians also adopted Eastern orthodoxy.

The medieval state of Kiev in the Ukraine became Christian when its Grand Prince Vladimir accepted Christianity for himself and his people in 987 and married the Byzantine Princess Anna. Vladimir had already received Christian instruction from his grandmother, Princess Olga of Kiev, a Christian convert. Thus the Russian Church was a daughter of the Eastern Orthodox Church and remained under the jurisdiction of the patriarch of Constantinople until 1589. At that time the metropolitan of Moscow was given patriarchal rank and the Russian Church became independent. In the modern Soviet state this church is increasingly used for the political purposes of communism, though its spiritual life survives.

Chapter 25 Eastern Orthodoxy Today

The Eastern Church, after surviving the overthrow of the Byzantine Empire in 1453, entered upon five centuries of change, all the while clinging to its own worship and faith. Dogma was of less concern in the East than religious experience. This was sought through worship that aimed to bring the faithful into mystical touch with God. The creeds were regarded less as statements of belief than as acts of worship. By the 13th century the Byzantine rite, which was developed at Constantinople, became the standard among the Orthodox and was adapted and translated from its original Greek into the many languages of the various Eastern churches. With the appearance of autonomous national churches, the community of the Eastern Orthodox Church came into being. It derives its theological unity from the acceptance of the decrees of the seven ecumenical councils held between 325 and 787.

Despite the fact that today this communion regards itself as the true heir of the Early Christian Church, it has been able to establish friendly contacts with other Christian bodies, and many of its churches are members of the World Council of Churches. The Eastern Church consists of the four ancient patriarchates of Constantinople, Alexandria, Antioch, Jerusalem, as well as the Orthodox Churches of Cyprus, Russia, Rumania, Yugoslavia, Greece, Bulgaria, Georgia, Albania, Finland, and Czechoslovakia. The Ecumenical Patriarch of Constantinople leads the Eastern Orthodox communion, but his jurisdiction in the East is not comparable to that of the pope in the West, for the patriarch is regarded as the "first among equals," and he directly controls only his own church. Many of the members of his church live in the Americas and Europe.

Nourished by the sacraments and inspired by the liturgy, the study of the Scriptures, and the example of monastic life, Christianity has survived many attacks and continues as a potent force in the East. Today, many of its churches and monasteries, with their marvelous mosaic and fresco decorations in which time and eternity seem to mingle, bear visible witness to the living traditions of Christianity in the East.

Part Six
The Reformation 1500-1600

Chapter 26 The Winds of Change

During the Middle Ages, Christianity spread throughout Europe. The church, as we have noted, moved into the vacuum created by the fall of the Roman Empire and took upon itself the tasks of civilization. It gave people standards of conduct. It preached peace and reconciliation. During the misery and insecurity of the Middle Ages it inspired a transcendent hope that sustained the lives of ordinary people. It preserved many of the skills and much of the learning of ancient Greece and Rome. It converted the barbarians and welcomed them into the Christian family. Finally, the church established a new and all-embracing unity in Europe.

Over the church in the West the bishop of Rome, the pope, reigned as supreme lawgiver and judge, though not without opposition. He confirmed the election of all bishops, controlled the clergy and the monasteries, sent his legates to the royal courts, and claimed temporal power over emperors, kings, and other rulers. Using his financial powers, he assessed the various ecclesiastical dioceses and districts, charged fees for certain services, and levied upon every Christian household the small annual tax called Peter's Pence. By his authority to excommunicate, to deny the sacraments and fellowship of the church to individuals or even to entire nations, he acquired great power.

The church declared that it alone could interpret the teachings of Jesus Christ and save souls for eternity. Outside the church no one could be saved. Consequently, during the Middle Ages the life of every man, woman, and child was dominated by the church. Nevertheless, opposition to the power of the clergy and to canon law began to grow among business people and laymen in the professions and the royal councils.

By the middle of the 14th century the winds of change began to blow. Ecclesiastically, politically, economically, culturally, and intellectually, the established order was in transition. Feudalism, doomed by the economic burdens of the Crusades and the devastating wars of the Middle Ages, was being replaced by national states in which the common people were gaining a voice. Serfdom, undermined by the new money economy, was disappearing. With the emerging power of the middle class and the expansion of trade and industry, medieval towns were growing in size and importance. The frail boats of the Middle Ages were being replaced by more seaworthy ships that could navigate in the open ocean and, by the use of the newly introduced astrolabe and compass, return safely to their home ports.

The church, which had presided over most of the great medieval achievements in scholarship, art, and literature and had trained the outstanding minds of the period, continued to nurture scholars and artists of many kinds. Throughout the Renaissance—that rich development of western civilization from the 14th to the 17th century—the church became the patron of outstanding triumphs of art, literature, and learning. Many of the early humanists, the scholars of the "new learning," were churchmen.

The "new learning" was greatly stimulated by the fall of Constantinople to the Ottoman Turks in 1453, when

Greek scholars, bringing their precious books of the Greek and Roman classics with them, fled to the West. After rediscovering the treasures of ancient culture, the humanists turned away from the abstract speculations of scholasticism in their enthusiasm for classical ideas and forms and for all that was natural and human. When the great classics of Greece and Rome became popular in the universities of Europe, some churchmen feared that they might overshadow the moral teachings of Christianity. But bishops as well as princes gradually accepted the "new learning." In the middle of the 15th century, Pope Nicholas V, a renowned classical scholar himself, founded the Vatican Library and established the papacy as the patron of classical studies. Many humanists began to turn their attention to the early writings of Christianity and to study the Bible from a fresh viewpoint. This was to revolutionize the religious outlook of Western Europe and prepare the way for the Reformation.

Toward the end of the Middle Ages all these changes produced a creative upheaval that signaled the arrival of a new era in human development. There was an upsurge of confidence in human beings and in the infinite range of their possibilities. Increasing attention was focused on the dignity and worth of individual men and women—a basic teaching of Christianity, which was expressed in the church's concern for human welfare.

Concrete evidences of the dawn of a new era abound in the 14th and 15th centuries. As early as 1382, as was noted in a previous section, Wycliffe, who was called "the morning star of the Reformation," brought the Bible to the common people of England. Though the time was not yet ripe for his teachings, he planted a seed that, despite official persecution and the lack of efficient means of communicating ideas, would finally bear a harvest.

The invention of printing proved to be a powerful factor

in the Reformation. The first substantial work produced from moveable metal type in the western world was the Latin Bible printed on Gutenberg's press in Mainz on the Rhine about 1455. In England, twenty years later, William Caxton was encouraged to set up his press and print his first book in the almonry of Westminster Abbey, thanks to the interest and patronage of a remarkable woman, Lady Margaret Beaufort, a descendant of Edward III and the mother of Henry VII.

With the pattern of medieval life slowly changing, people began to protest against abuses that had crept into their religious institutions and to question superstitions that had long been taken for granted. Many of the religious forms that had once nurtured their spirits had become empty formulas unable to satisfy their inner life. The church needed to adjust itself to the world around it. The church needed to reform. Unfortunately, the church was so closely involved with the politics and power of the state that when the Reformation arrived it caused violence—a violence that shattered the medieval unity of the church.

Chapter 27 Desiderius Erasmus
1466-1536

Erasmus, a Dutch humanist, became one of the most influential men of his day and a precursor of the Reformation. Though born in Rotterdam, he spent most of his life in France, England, Italy, Germany, and Switzerland, for he was a universal man who, in his own words, "treated the world as the common country of us all." As a boy of nine he attended a school in Deventer where his exceptional promise showed itself in an extraordinary memory and a passion for learning. One of his schoolfellows, Adrian of Utrecht, became tutor to Emperor Charles V and eventually pope. As Adrian VI, he tried to check moral and administrative evils, but died in less than two years. He was the last non-Italian pope until John Paul II was elected in 1978.

When Erasmus was about eighteen, following the death of his mother and father, he was forced by poverty to enter a monastery where he spent much time in the library studying its few books. Monastic life, however, with all its chapel-going and other routines, bored him, for he found no one of his own intellectual ability to talk to. He finally gained freedom from his monastic obligations and studied at the University of Paris. To support himself, he began to teach.

Among his pupils was Lord Mountjoy, who invited him to England and introduced him to the remarkable group of humanists at Oxford. They based their teaching on the classics and the Bible, believing that these would throw new light on old truths. As the following excerpt from one of his letters reveals, Erasmus was charmed with everybody and everything he saw in England.

> The air is soft and delicious. The men are sensible and intelligent. Many of them are even learned. . . . They know their classics. . . . When Colet speaks I might be listening to Plato. Linacre [later physician to Henry VIII] is as deep and acute a thinker as I have ever met with. Grocyn is a mine of knowledge; and nature never formed a sweeter and happier disposition than that of Thomas More. The number of young men who are studying ancient literature here is astonishing.

These new friends, all of whom were to become eminent, stimulated his interest in the classics. John Colet, having studied in Italy and France, was lecturing to crowds of Oxford students on the life and letters of Paul. Because Colet believed that it was necessary to return to Biblical sources, he persuaded Erasmus to study Greek and devote himself to the New Testament in its original language. Later Erasmus wrote to Colet saying, "You are trying to bring back the Christianity of the apostles, and clear away the thorns and briars with which it is overgrown—a noble undertaking."

When, in 1501, Erasmus visited England again, Thomas More, then only twenty-two, took him to the palace at Eltham near Greenwich where the royal children were often sent for a change of air. Though King Henry VII, his queen, and his eldest son, Arthur, were absent, Erasmus met Prince Henry and his two sisters: Margaret, later Queen of Scotland and grandmother of Mary Queen of Scots; and three-year-old Mary, who was briefly to be Queen of France and subsequently grandmother of Lady Jane Grey. Erasmus was impressed by the gentle yet regal bearing of Prince Henry, a gifted, well-educated boy of nine who had been told of his guest's intellectual brilliance

Desiderius Erasmus, 1466-1536

The New York Public Library, Prints Division

Desiderius Erasmus—Frans Lys (1601)

This engraving, from a portrait by Hans Holbein the younger of his good friend Erasmus in old age, shows the famous scholar and writer with his ornate Bible beside him and, in the background, his native Rotterdam and the dike-protected Dutch coast.

and was eager to hear him talk. Later, when the prince was fifteen, he replied to a letter he had received from Erasmus, writing, "Your letter charms me, most eloquent Erasmus, . . . but it is not for me to commend a style which all the world praises."

Because of his wisdom, his wit, his books, his large correspondence, and his scholarly work, Erasmus became widely known in Europe. Through his common sense and his rationality in religion, he exemplified all that was best in European humanism. He knew and wrote to most of the men of learning of his time, and many rulers, including Charles V, Pope Leo X, and Henry VIII, recognized his influence and sought his counsel.

The bulk of his work consisted of editions of the Church Fathers—Jerome, Cyprian, Irenaeus, Ambrose, Augustine, Chrysostom, Basil, Origen. These texts, with the prefaces he wrote for them, were printed by the famous early printer John Froben at Basel.

The most important work of Erasmus, however, was his edition of the Greek text of the New Testament, with his Latin translation of that text and his notes on the contents. When the book was issued in 1516—the first printed New Testament to appear in the original Greek—it was dedicated to Pope Leo X, who had approved of the undertaking. Erasmus had worked on this New Testament between 1511 and 1514 while occupying the Lady Margaret Beaufort chair of Divinity at Cambridge, which his friend John Fisher had secured for him.

Erasmus's New Testament became overwhelmingly successful, a hundred thousand copies being immediately sold in France alone. In subsequent editions his notes and comments on the text were expanded and became more outspoken against abuses in the church and the ignorance of lay people. In the 16th century the Bible was often used as an occasion for broadcasting the opinions of the translator.

Up to this time copies of the Bible had been shut up in monastic libraries, where only theologians had access to them. Lay people knew only the selections they heard in church, but, as these were in Latin and often read unintelligibly, the Bible failed to communicate its message. In the New Testament that Erasmus made available, Greek scholars and other educated people could now discover for themselves the facts of Christ, the apostles, and their teachings. They could compare the imperfect and often debased life of the church of their day with the Christianity that had converted the world. The result was a spiritual earthquake.

"My work," Erasmus wrote in 1521, "has been to restore a buried literature, and recall divines from their hair-splittings to a knowledge of the New Testament." Knowledge of the Scriptures was one of the basic principles of the Reformation.

Besides his work as an editor, Erasmus was always engaged in writing some book or pamphlet in his brilliant, humorous, flexible style. His vast learning and deep concern for the troubles of Christendom, combined with his transparent honesty and his lucid style of writing, captured the attention of his contemporaries. He wrote, of course, in Latin, the common language of scholars and educated people throughout Europe. The dialogues in his *Colloquies* satirize the corruptions of society with wit and compassion. His *Adages* reveal his opinions on current issues. His best-known book, *The Praise of Folly*, sums up conversations he had while visiting his English friends, Thomas More, then in the king's service, and John Fisher, bishop of Rochester. With bitter earnestness, the three friends discussed the tragedy of the church and heaped scorn on its evils and abuses.

His hope was that as people became better informed and more intelligent, they would recognize and quietly outgrow their own weaknesses and the evils, superstitions, and empty practices of the church. Viewing the storm aroused by Luther's movement, he warned, "Of course the church requires reform, but violence is not the way to it." It still seemed possible to him that, with men of learning occupying the thrones of Europe, the time was ripe for quiet reform. This, however, was not to be.

Chapter 28 Martin Luther
1483-1546

The spark that ignited the Reformation was the act of an Augustinian monk, Biblical scholar, and professor of theology at the University of Wittenberg, Martin Luther. His father was a devout peasant miner who, having struggled through poverty to become a fairly prosperous townsman, was ambitious for his son to be a lawyer. Luther entered the university, but a haunting sense of his own sinfulness made him renounce the world to become a monk. A man of unusual piety and monastic zeal, he showed remarkable gifts for preaching, for teaching, and for the practical matters of administration.

During a period of inner conflict, when all his rigorous ascetic practices and spiritual "works" failed to bring him a sense of being close to God, he began to doubt that the church possessed the means of salvation. Was God's favor to be won by earning merit through the sacraments and the "good works" required by the church? Suddenly, Paul's statement in Romans 1.17 struck Luther like a thunderbolt: "The just shall live by faith," or, "He who through faith is righteous shall live." He said that the passage became for him "the true gate of Paradise," and henceforth, instead of struggling to earn his salvation by his own efforts, he rested upon the faith that God had given him. From this personal experience Luther developed a doctrine contrary to the church's teaching of "justification by sacraments and works." He preached that God's gift of faith is the only condition of salvation, of being freed from human guilt and sin and made righteous before God.

His conflict with the church began when agents from Pope Leo X arrived in Germany to sell "indulgences"— papal pardons that remitted part of a person's suffering in purgatory for sins he or she had already repented of and done penance for. These were issued in order to raise money for the rebuilding of St. Peter's in Rome, the central church of western Christendom. Luther regarded the selling of indulgences as a scandalous abuse that was contrary to the deepest truths of Christianity. Accordingly, on October 31st, 1517, he wrote ninety-five statements that challenged the granting of indulgences. These were the famous ninety-five theses that he nailed to the door of the castle church at Wittenberg. He aimed for discussion leading to reform—not revolt. The discussion never took place, but the theses were widely circulated and eagerly read. The time was ripe, passions were aroused, and drastic actions were taken. Luther had precipitated the greatest revolution in the history of the church.

He continued to speak and write against ecclesiastical abuses and against the divine authority of the church itself, even urging the German princes to free their states from foreign papal control. Summoned before the Diet, or assembly of states of the Holy Roman Empire, that met at Worms in 1521, he acknowledged that he had written the pile of German and Latin works his judges showed him, but he declared that he could not recant what he had said against the pope unless adequate arguments against his position could be found in the Scriptures. "I cannot do otherwise," he cried. "Here I stand. God help me. Amen."

The Diet now issued an edict declaring Luther an outlaw and forbidding anyone to give him food, drink, or shelter. So popular, however, had Luther's teachings become that he was already a hero, and few people paid any attention to the Edict of Worms. Immediately his friends found a safe haven for him at Wartburg, in the castle of Frederick the Wise, elector of Saxony.

While in hiding at Wartburg, Luther translated the New Testament into German and published it in 1522. He did not base his version on the Vulgate, from which the earlier and somewhat awkward German versions had been made, but translated instead the Greek text now available in printed form, thanks to the labors of Erasmus. During the next ten years, in addition to organizing and spreading his new teachings, he completed his translation of the entire Bible. This epoch-making version was both a religious and a literary treasure, for Luther had become a master of popular expression. His translation was readable, idiomatic, and polished. The pattern of speech of future German literature was largely set by Luther's Bible.

The revolt in the German states against the papacy was joined by pious people shocked by the abuses of the church, by worldly people eager to seize church lands and revenues, and by patriots anxious to be free from domination by Rome. Princes, burghers, artisans, peasants, and many clergymen joined Luther's cause. He and his supporters attacked the whole system of spiritual domination, with its pardons, excommunications, dispensations, absolutions, as well as the confessional, and the ecclesiastical courts. Soon violence erupted and Germany was in turmoil.

Erasmus watched from afar and expressed his dismay that his teachings, as Luther and others used them, had produced such appalling results. At first, Erasmus wrote that he "approved of what seemed good in his [Luther's] work. I told him in a letter that if he would moderate his language he might be a shining light, and that the pope, I did not doubt, would be his friend." But later he declared, "I can be no party to violence." His concern deepened as the revolt in Germany became more bitter. "What could have induced him to rail as he did at popes and doctors and mendicant friars?" asked Erasmus. "Things were bad enough in themselves without making them worse. Did he wish to set the world on fire?"

At the Diet of Speyer in 1529 a majority of the rulers of the various German states decided to act against Luther, but the minority, having adopted Lutheran reforms, signed a protest. Because of this the Lutheran rulers were called *Protestants*, a name now generally given to those who do not accept the teachings and rule of the Roman Catholic Church.

In 1530 Luther's learned friend and colleague at Wittenberg, the gentle humanist Philip Melanchthon, prepared an orderly statement of the beliefs and doctrines of Lutherans that is now called the Augsburg Confession. After its acceptance by the Lutheran princes of Germany it became the chief creed of the Lutheran Church. With this standard of belief, with a German Bible, and with worship enriched by congregational singing, all in the everyday language of the German people, the Lutheran Church grew rapidly. It spread to the kingdoms of Sweden, Denmark, and Norway, in all of which it became the established religion. Germany itself remained divided into Roman Catholic and Lutheran states because the religion of the ruler usually determined the religion of his people.

Luther spent the rest of his life organizing and spreading his new gospel. In 1525 he married a former nun, Katherine von Bora, a worthy helpmate who provided a happy family life for him with their three sons and two daughters.

Among his other concerns he found time to write more than thirty hymns, one of which, *Ein' Feste Burg*, "A mighty fortress is our God," is sung in Protestant churches everywhere as a battle cry of faith. Luther probably developed its melody from an old Gregorian chant. The entire hymn, and especially its first line, which is engraved on his monument at Wittenberg, seems to convey the ruggedness and strength of Luther himself.

Chapter 29 John Calvin
1509-1564

Next to Martin Luther, the most conspicuous leader of Protestantism in the 16th century was the French theologian John Calvin. The two men displayed opposite temperaments, Luther being impulsive, creative, and emotional, while Calvin was ascetic, calm, reasonable, and logical. Calvin was born into a prosperous, middle-class family living in Noyon, northeast of Paris. His father planned a career in the Catholic Church for his son and obtained a church benefice for him. This enabled young Calvin to study at the University of Paris where he immersed himself in humanist studies and developed a brilliant style of writing. On the advice of his relative, Olivetan, the first translator of the Bible into French, Calvin studied the Scriptures and learned to read the New Testament in Greek. As Luther's ideas were beginning to influence many people in France at this time, Calvin soon found himself in a group of humanists who disagreed with the practices and doctrines of the church.

While in his early twenties he experienced what he reported as "a sudden conversion" in which he became deeply convinced that God spoke to him through the Scriptures and that from now on he must obey God's will. Realizing that he could no longer remain in the Catholic Church, he gave up the income from his benefice. Because his break with the church made France unsafe for him, he moved to Basel, the Protestant city and university center in northern Switzerland where Froben had printed the Greek text of the New Testament prepared by Erasmus.

In Basel, in 1536, Calvin published his famous *Institutes of the Christian Religion,* which has been called the summa of classical Protestantism. Beautifully written, this restrained statement presented the theological ideas of earlier leaders, especially Luther and the Swiss reformer Ulrich Zwingli, in a clear and logical way. Calvin rejected papal authority, accepted such doctrines as the infallibility of the Bible, justification by faith alone, and predestination. He also approved of church discipline for maintaining the moral purity of the faithful. Calvin's *Institutes,* which he dedicated to the king of France in a dignified, courteous letter, made him, at the age of twenty-six, the leader of French Protestantism.

Invited by the French reformer Guillaume Farel to help to organize the new Protestant republic in Geneva, Calvin moved to that Swiss city in 1536. Except for a brief exile, he held the commanding position of chief pastor and preacher in Geneva until his death. The city, under his religious and political leadership, became the nursery of Protestantism in western Europe, and he was referred to as the "Protestant pope." He constructed a theocratic state whose civil affairs were guided by the church. The church was managed by its ministers and elders, or *presbyters,* from whom the word "Presbyterian" was derived. Calvin emphasized the virtues of thrift, industry, sobriety, and responsibility, all of which he believed were essential to the achievement of God's reign on earth.

Calvin not only preached every day and ruled on matters of doctrine and church government, but he was also consulted on questions of law, police, economy, trade, and manufactures. He carried on a large correspondence, wrote theological treatises as well as commentaries on the Scriptures, and issued a French translation of the Bible. He founded schools and the University of Geneva, which attracted students from England, Scotland, and many parts of Europe, thus spreading Calvinism far and wide.

English scholars, fleeing from Queen Mary's persecutions, found in Geneva the freedom and encouragement they needed to revise the Great Bible of 1539 according to improved standards of scholarship. Calvin's brother-in-law, William Whittingham, an Oxford scholar, is credited with the preparation and printing of the Geneva New Testament of 1557. Three years later the entire Geneva Bible was completed—the most accurate and extensively annotated of the six English Bibles that had so far been printed. Its relatively small size and the division of its chapters into verses made it convenient to use. It became the popular family Bible, the version read by Shakespeare, and the version brought to America by the pilgrims.

The men whom Calvin trained in Geneva carried his principles to almost every country in Europe, establishing a puritan standard of behavior among Protestants. In Scotland, in 1560, despite the resistance of Mary Queen of Scots, John Knox organized a national Reformed Church whose members were called Presbyterians. The Calvinists of France were called Huguenots. In the Netherlands, Calvinism became the religion of the patriots, who, under William of Orange, established the Dutch Republic. English Calvinists were called Presbyterians and those who wanted to further purify the church of Catholic elements were called Puritans. Many of these emigrated to Massachusetts in the 17th century. Calvinism, through its intellectual life, its steadfast piety, and its active social involvement, permanently influenced European culture from Calvin's time to today.

Chapter 30 The English Church and Henry VIII
1509-1547

By the beginning of the 16th century many of the English people had become discontented with the church. Popular feeling against it had been growing rapidly since John Wycliffe's time in the late 14th century. There were numerous grounds for dissatisfaction. The English were the most nationalist of European people and their distrust of the church rested partly on a political dislike for the foreign papacy. As early as 1215 the English barons had forced the Magna Charta upon the reluctant King John. This most important document of British constitutional history contains a declaration aimed against both royal autocracy and papal interference: "The Church of England shall be free to have her rights and liberties uninjured."

During the Middle Ages some clergymen were so poorly educated that they did not understand the Latin words of the Bible. The higher clergy, on the other hand, were wealthy, privileged, and powerful. Bishops lived in palaces like princes. The church owned one quarter of the land and controlled at least a tenth of the national income, yet paid no taxes. Huge sums of money were sent to Rome for papal purposes, thus causing resentment especially among the poor and the middle class. People complained about church fees and taxes, were critical of the lives and morals of some of the clergy, and displeased by what they saw in the monasteries, many of which had clearly outlived the purposes for which they were established. Added to all this was the influence of the leading humanists of the early 16th century, Erasmus, Colet, Thomas More, and others at Oxford and Cambridge who advocated reform of the church and a return to the pure Christianity of the Scriptures.

Despite some criticism of the church, the English continued to be a devout people whose church bells were seldom silent, giving the land the reputation of being "the ringing isle." Church building continued up to the time of the Reformation. Bath Abbey, as we see it today, was begun by Henry VII's master masons in 1499. The superlatively beautiful great vault of King's College Chapel, Cambridge, was completed in 1513 and its glorious windows in 1531.

Henry VIII was a devoted Catholic, versed in theology, brilliant, well-educated, and not entirely frivolous. When, in 1521, he learned of the new Lutheran heresy in Germany, he was shocked and wrote a book against it, *The Defense of the Seven Sacraments.* He sent a copy of this book with a dedicatory letter to Pope Leo X. In view of later events, it is ironic that Henry's chancellor, Sir Thomas More, advised the king not to emphasize the pope's authority too much in the letter. Brushing aside More's caution, Henry exclaimed, "We are so much bounden to the See of Rome that we cannot do too much honor to it."

The pope, gratified by Henry's respect and the soundness of his doctrines, conferred upon him the title *Fidei Defensor,* Defender of the Faith, a title he bore until his death. The sovereigns of Great Britain continue to bear this title, and it appears on modern British coins in the form "F D" or "Fid Def."

The political situation in which Henry was involved now began to push him inexorably toward a break with the papacy. He questioned the validity of his marriage to Catherine of Aragon, who had been the wife of his deceased brother, Arthur. Church law forbade marriage to a brother's widow and Henry's marriage had required a papal dispensation. Catherine had borne Henry only one living child, Princess Mary, and it appeared unlikely that she would bear him the son he needed to succeed him. To avoid a civil war over the succession, like the late War of the Roses, Henry knew that he must have a legitimate male heir. A woman had never ruled England. Margaret Beaufort's obvious claim to the throne had recently been passed over in favor of her son, Henry VII, as had the claim of his wife, Elizabeth of York. It was therefore not entirely the king's infatuation with Anne Boleyn but political wisdom as well that prompted Henry to ask the pope for an annulment of his marriage with Catherine on the basis that the dispensation of the previous pope had been unjustified. Though such an annulment was not unusual, Pope Clement VII took no action on Henry's petition for seven years. This was apparently because, since the sack of Rome in 1527, he was being held virtually a prisoner of war by Emperor Charles V, and Charles was determined that his aunt, Queen Catherine, should not be set aside by Henry.

The king, by now resentful of the pope's inaction and his evident disregard for England's best interests, took matters into his own hands. He dismissed Cardinal Wolsey, his chief minister, because of his failure to obtain an annulment of the royal marriage and gave the great seal to Sir Thomas More. Beginning in 1529, both Parliament and Convocation, which was the assembly of the English bishops and clergy, passed a series of laws, petitions, and resolutions indicating support for a break in relations with the papacy. In 1534 Convocation declared that "the Bishop of Rome hath not by Scripture any greater authority in England than any other foreign bishop." Parliament, in the same year, forbade sending further payments to the pope and directed that the archbishop of Canterbury issue all future dispensations and licenses. This law, however, expressly stated that it was not to be interpreted as changing any doctrine of the ancient Catholic faith. Thus the Reformation began in England with no change in the church except freedom from papal control. The Church of England continued as the Catholic Church of the centuries.

The former powers exercised by the pope in England were now divided between the church and the sovereign. The archbishop of Canterbury became the highest ecclesiastical authority in England for purely religious matters; the king became responsible, as Christian princes of that era usually were, for managing the outward affairs of the church—its rights, welfare, and peace.

Henry nominated Thomas Cranmer, a Cambridge scholar long opposed to papal power, to be archbishop of Canterbury. After his election and consecration in 1533, Cranmer summoned an ecclesiastical court and pronounced the king's marriage to Catherine invalid. Thereupon, Henry married Anne Boleyn, who bore him a daughter, Elizabeth.

On November 3, 1534, Parliament passed the Act of Supremacy by which Henry and his successors were declared "only supreme head on earth of the Church of England, as far as the law of Christ allows." Those who denied the king's supremacy were subject to punishment for high treason, which was beheading. Two leading scholars and churchmen of outstanding character, Bishop John Fisher of Rochester, whom Erasmus had called a "saint," and Sir Thomas More, whom he greatly admired as "a true friend," were committed to the Tower for denying the king's supremacy. When the pope reacted to this by making Fisher a cardinal, both he and More were beheaded. Henry's own daughter, Mary, refused to renounce the pope, but probably unknown to her, Cranmer interceded for her and saved her from the block.

The new pope, Paul III, excommunicated Henry and ordered the English people to revolt against him. He also urged the sovereigns of Europe to make war on him. In

England there were minor protests against the king, like the Pilgrimage of Grace in the north. On the whole, however, the pope's call was disregarded, and the English Church went on its way with the Mass, the sacraments, and the services virtually unchanged.

Yet there was one aspect of church life that experienced violent change. Henry and his chief minister, the unscrupulous politician Thomas Cromwell, greedy for monastic lands and wealth, ruthlessly suppressed the monasteries. Their excuse was that these were directly responsible to the pope and centers of the evils in the church that needed reform. Because these institutions had clearly outlived their former usefulness, few voices were raised in their defense. But by their destruction Cromwell changed the face of England. Lead was stripped from the roofs of magnificent old abbeys, which then decayed, becoming "bare ruined choirs." Stone, timber, and brick were salvaged from the suppressed monasteries by townsmen and squires for their own use. Some of the splendid old abbey churches, like the one at Tewkesbury, barely escaped destruction. When the monastery at Tewkesbury was dissolved and its church declared "superfluous," the resolute townsfolk claimed that the nave had always been their parish church. They were allowed to buy the entire great Norman structure for 450 English pounds, the estimated value of the bells and lead roof, which Cromwell's commissioners intended to melt down and sell.

Henry rewarded his friends and supporters with the former monastery lands or sold them at low prices to the rising classes, but he kept a few of the lands for his own use. The most notable of these were the tracts that later became the chief parks of London.

In addition to the destruction of the monasteries, Cromwell's agents and the iconoclasts of Edward VI's reign, in their blind zeal to sweep away all evidences of outworn beliefs and superstitions, caused much of the beauty of medieval England to perish. They smashed venerated images and the lacy stonework surrounding them. They hurled stones through stained glass windows that depicted saints and angels. They scattered the relics of saints and the shrines in which they were kept. Edward the Confessor's jeweled, wonder-working shrine in Westminister Abbey was pulled apart and desecrated. Thomas à Becket's golden pilgrimage shrine in Canterbury was completely destroyed.

Despite these transformations, the religious life and habits of the people continued with little outward change. Secret supporters of the pope worshiped with their neighbors in the same parish churches and received the sacrament together at the same altars. Like their king, the majority of English people approved of the separation of the Church of England from papal control, but they did not desire to adopt the radical alterations in doctrine or worship that Luther and Calvin had introduced on the continent.

Nevertheless, changes were inevitably taking place. For centuries the people had been taught that the pope alone possessed the keys that unlock the gates of heaven. With the pope gone, they asked, "Who now has power to remit our sins and save our souls?" As early as 1536 Archbishop Cranmer answered this question forthrightly. No man and no human institution, he explained, could obtain salvation for them. It was wrong, he said, to attribute "the remission of our sins to any laws or ceremonies of man's making." Only by their faith in Christ could they obtain their own salvation. Thus, Protestant doctrines began to be taught in the English Church.

At the very heart of the Reformation was the Bible. As we have seen, scholars devoted themselves to studying it in its original languages. Everywhere, movements were under way to translate it into the new national languages so that lay people might discover for themselves the meaning of

God's Word. In England, however, severe laws still forbade lay people to read the Scriptures. Moreover, until William Tyndale's New Testament appeared in 1525, no version of it existed in the language English people were now speaking.

Thanks to Tyndale's training in classical scholarship at Oxford under Grocyn, Latimer, and Linacre, and at Cambridge under Erasmus; thanks to his superb command of the emerging modern English language; and thanks also to the heroic efforts of Tyndale and his followers, some of whom forfeited their lives in the cause; English people were finally provided with a Bible in their own tongue. Though the authorities feared the Protestant ideas expressed in Tyndale's introductions and marginal notes, and made bonfires of as many copies of his Bible as they could collect, they could not stem the flow of copies printed in Germany and shipped to the English ports. Nor could they restrain public demand for this epoch-making version.

Shortly before Tyndale's martyrdom near Brussels in 1535, Miles Coverdale issued the first complete printed English Bible. For this he gathered and edited some of the best translations he could find, many of them Tyndale's. He dedicated the volume to Henry VIII, who is depicted on the title page. In 1537 John Rogers, Tyndale's literary executor, issued a compilation of all of Tyndale's New Testament and Old Testament translations, completing the Bible with some of Coverdale's work and issuing it under the pseudonym of Thomas Matthew. The Matthew Bible became the basis of subsequent English versions. Both Cranmer and Cromwell welcomed this Bible and Cromwell obtained royal authority for it, making it legal "to be bought and read within this realm."

Shrewd politician that he was, Cromwell perceived the inadequacies of the two English Bibles then circulating: Matthew's carried controversial Protestant notes; Coverdale's was of uneven quality. Cromwell therefore obtained the king's approval to prepare the Great Bible of 1593 and issue it in a handsome folio volume. It largely consisted of Tyndale's superb translations as edited by Coverdale, but without the controversial notes. Henry's chief minister then ordered this Bible to be set up in parish churches everywhere so that people might read the Word of God in English.

At the end of his reign, Henry bequeathed to his son a realm in which the great majority of the people supported the Church of England. On either side of this majority were two smaller parties. The Protestants, who had been increasing despite Henry's repression, desired to introduce Lutheran and Calvinistic reforms. The Catholic faction aimed to restore the power of the papacy. In the reign of Edward VI the Protestants would gain power. In Mary's reign the Catholics would be in control.

Chapter 31   The Reigns of Edward VI and Mary
1547-1558

Edward VI, son of Henry VIII and his third wife, Jane Seymour, came to the throne of England as a serious, gravelooking little boy of nine. At his coronation, when the three swords representing his three kingdoms were presented to him, he is reported to have asked for a fourth—the Bible— calling it, as he may have been instructed to do, "the Sword of the Spirit . . . to be preferred before these other swords." During his six-year reign, while England became more and more Protestant, Edward gained an intelligent understanding of the affairs of both church and state.

Edward's council chose his uncle, the Duke of Somerset, a man of action and a brilliant soldier, to be protector of the realm during Edward's childhood. Somerset, with his Protestant sympathies and good intentions, believed in both religious and political liberty and was a friend to the poor and dispossessed. Nevertheless, he was a man of his time, and also personally ambitious for wealth and power. In order to secure building materials for his own palace he pulled down an aisle of St. Paul's and planned to pull down Westminister Abbey, until he was dissuaded by its dean. By giving the radical Protestant reformers a free hand to change the religious customs of England, he unleashed bitter dissension and even popular uprisings.

At this time Thomas Cranmer, the scholarly archbishop of Canterbury, believing that new religious laws and regulations could not accomplish true reform of the church, set about the task of revising the worship and sacraments of the medieval church. In 1549 he and others introduced the First Prayer Book of Edward VI in an attempt to restore the spirit of worship of the early Christians. He translated the old services from their medieval Latin into English, made them simpler, removed superstitious references, and restored Bible readings to their central place in the services.

From Coverdale's poetic version of the psalms to Cranmer's concise yet eloquent and expressive collects, it was an English masterpiece. It survived the religious upheavals of the next century with remarkably few changes and set the tone of Anglican worship. From now on people could understand the words of church services and take an intelligent part in the worship of God. At this time Cranmer also prepared a statement of faith designed both to exclude current heretical ideas and to serve as a basis for unity. Called the *Forty-two Articles*, this document was authorized by the young king just before he died in 1553.

Edward's successor was his older half-sister, Mary, a devout Catholic who was the daughter of Catherine of Aragon. During the five years of her reign, she restored papal authority in England and revived the medieval laws against heresy. She requested Cardinal Reginald Pole, a member of the royal family who had lived abroad for many years, to return to England as papal legate. He sailed triumphantly up the Thames in a barge whose prow was decorated with a gleaming cross. After addressing Parliament, he administered absolution to the whole nation, thus freeing the kingdom from its guilt of schism and heresy. Pole, however, was too unrealistic and out of touch with English life to help Mary deal with Protestantism and stem its advance.

Mary's marriage to Philip II of Spain, the outstanding champion of Catholicism in Europe, brought her personal unhappiness, proved to be unpopular with the English people, and did not advance the Catholic cause.

Finally, seeing no other way of restoring England to the Roman Church, Mary and her advisers resorted to persecution. Nearly three hundred English reformers perished, many of them by fire, because the queen believed that only fire could purge England of their heinous offenses.

John Rogers, a canon of St. Paul's and Tyndale's friend and literary executor, was the first martyr to die in the fires of Smithfield on the outskirts of London. With a London crowd cheering him, his journey to the stake became a triumphant procession.

Opposite the gate of Balliol College in Oxford, on October 16, 1555, Hugh Latimer and Nicholas Ridley, two saintly men and well-known reformers, were burned at the stake. With his last words, Latimer encouraged Ridley, saying, "Be of good comfort, Master Ridley, and play the man; we shall this day light such a candle by God's grace in England as, I trust, shall never be put out." Latimer, royal chaplain and adviser of Henry VIII, by his witty, vigorous preaching and his profound religious feeling, had won many to the principles of the Reformation. Ridley, bishop of London, had served the needy in his diocese and established discipline among his clergy.

The next year, Thomas Cranmer, by now aged and frail, was degraded from his office of archbishop. At his trial he recanted, his chief weakness being, as Bishop Hooper of Gloucester had noted, that he was "too fearful about what might happen to him." Despite his recantation, he was condemned to death at Oxford. At the stake he prayed for God's forgiveness and heroically stretched out to the flames the hand that had signed his recantation, exclaiming, "This unworthy right hand."

The violent means Mary used to stamp out heresy offended the sensibilities of the English people and proved that many in England, from saintly and learned bishops to ordinary men and women, were willing to die for their faith. Indeed, Latimer's candle could not be put out.

Chapter 32 The Elizabethan Settlement

Elizabeth I, after surviving the dangerous political and religious crosscurrents of her childhood and youth, succeeded her half-sister Mary in 1558 at the age of twenty-five and entered London to a tumultuous welcome. Her many portraits depict her as a remote, almost legendary figure, loaded with ornaments and jewels and dressed in extravagant gowns. During her forty-five year reign, however, she exercised an intelligent, tough-minded statesmanship that made England economically and politically powerful, and she largely healed its religious strife.

As the daughter of Anne Boleyn and Henry VIII, the queen was committed to separation from the Roman Church. Moreover, she had been exceptionally well-educated by tutors imbued with the new Christian learning of the Renaissance, and her ablest and most loyal subjects were Protestant. Among the first measures adopted in her reign was the Act of Supremacy, which established her, not as "supreme head" (a title distasteful to Catholics), but as "supreme governor of the Church of England."

The queen consulted with all groups concerning the welfare of the church and appointed a commission to revise the Prayer Book. In a spirit of conciliation, Cranmer's First and Second Prayer Books of 1549 and 1552 were worked together to form the *Book of Common Prayer* of 1559. This became the standard. It was a book whose English words could be understood by the people. It combined the essentials of Christian faith and practice with the new insights of the Reformation. It was based on the teachings of the Scriptures as interpreted both by the Fathers of the early church and by the new Christian learning. It embodied the historic Christian creeds; it preserved the sacraments of the ancient church; it recognized the traditional ministry of bishops, priests and deacons; and it made use of the missal, the breviary, and Eastern liturgies. For the first time, it made the entire liturgy of the church, with the exception of the lessons from the Bible, available to priests and lay people alike in a single volume. Finally, it expressed the Catholic faith in English words and phrases of such grace, harmony, and majesty that the language of prayer entered into the language of the people. An echo of the Prayer Book occurs in many a line of Shakespeare and in the poetry of such 17th-century poets as John Donne and George Herbert. Through the succeeding centuries the Prayer Book of 1559 provided the basis of worship in the Anglican Communion.

Though the Prayer Book as a whole contains the doctrine of the Church of England, a statement of its faith was issued in the *Thirty-nine Articles* of 1563—a revision of Cranmer's *Forty-two Articles* of a decade earlier. It dealt with the doctrinal disputes of the time in a moderate manner, so as to conciliate as many English people as possible.

Because most of the lower clergy had not been involved with Mary's politics, they continued their ministries under Elizabeth. It was different, however, with the bishops who had been consecrated in Mary's reign. All but one of them, after refusing to renounce their allegiance to the pope, gave up their dioceses, thus causing a great shortage of bishops.

At the death of Cardinal Pole, Elizabeth chose as the new archbishop of Canterbury her mother's one-time chaplain, Matthew Parker. He was a man of wisdom and steadiness of purpose and a former master of Corpus Christi College, Cambridge, where he is still remembered because each year on his birthday he was in the habit of presenting to the college a book from his library. He also bequeathed to the college his entire incomparable library of manuscripts and books collected from the dissolved monasteries in earlier years.

Matthew Parker's consecration on December 17, 1559, was planned with great care in order to preserve the apostolic succession of the English episcopate. At Lambeth Palace, the archbishop's residence on the Thames at London, beneath the five lancet windows in the old chapel where nearly two hundred years earlier John Wycliffe had been accused of heresy, Matthew Parker was consecrated by four bishops: William Barlow of Bath, John Scory of Hereford, John Hodgkin of Bedford, and Miles Coverdale, formerly of Exeter. Two of them had been consecrated in the reign of Henry VIII by the pre-Reformation rite. The other two had been consecrated according to the form incorporated in Cranmer's revised Prayer Book. Thus the historic succession of bishops since the days of the apostles was retained in the Church of England, and the validity of the Anglican orders of bishops, priests, and deacons established.

Not long after his consecration Archbishop Parker initiated a revision of the Great Bible in order to replace the popular Geneva Bible because it contained many controversial Calvinistic notes. In 1568, with the help of a group of revisers, Parker produced the Bishops' Bible in a large, handsome volume. Though its uneven quality was an obstacle to its popularity, it is important as the official basis of the King James, or Authorized Version of 1611.

In this period of passionate religious strife the various measures of the Elizabethan Settlement largely succeeded in unifying the religious life of England. By continuing the faith and practice of the ancient church, while accepting many of the truths that had emerged in the Reformation, the Church of England took a position between Roman Catholicism on one side and Lutheranism and Calvinism on the other. At this time the broad and inclusive Anglican doctrines and practices attained a permanent form that was to become basic in the world-encircling family of churches now belonging to the Anglican Communion.

The Anglican position was ably set forth and defended by two distinguished theological scholars: John Jewel and Richard Hooker. From his study of the tradition of the early Christian church, Jewel made a distinction between what are mere externals and what are truly the essentials of the church. While he was Bishop of Salisbury, he not only built up the ruined walls surrounding the cathedral close, but also, in a different kind of building, laid one of the foundation stones of Anglicanism. His *Apology for the Church of England*, written in 1562, for the first time systematically stated the position of the Church of England as it differed from that of the Church of Rome.

Richard Hooker, a poor boy from Heavitree near Exeter, with the help of Bishop John Jewel, was admitted to Corpus Christi College, Oxford. There he became one of England's great scholars. In the seclusion of the country parishes he later served, he wrote his monumental *Laws of Ecclesiastical Polity*, an epoch-making discussion of church government. This classic statement of Anglican principles, written in an excellent prose style, showed how the old and the new, the Catholic and the Reformed positions, could be reconciled and the historic continuity of the Church of England preserved. A marble statue of Hooker on the north side of the cathedral at Exeter depicts him, in his scholar's cap and gown, seated with an open book in his lap, as though watching over and guarding the ancient and the continuing life of the cathedral and the Christian community.

Despite basic differences, Anglican and Roman Catholics continued to worship together until 1570, thanks to the queen's policy of including within the national church as many English people with as wide a range of religious views as possible. Elizabeth did not regard the Church of England as a denomination or a sect, but as the whole nation at prayer.

In 1570 the pope excommunicated Elizabeth, ordered the Roman Catholics of England to withdraw from the Church of England, released the English people from their allegiance to the queen, and called upon the French and Spanish kings to invade the country. Among the conspiracies against the queen at this time, one involved her cousin, Mary Queen of Scots. A papal expedition supported an Irish rebellion, and preparations were begun for the Spanish Armada. During this period Elizabeth reacted by imprisoning or executing conspirators in what was partly religious persecution but also defense against treason.

On the other side of the Church of England were the Puritans, who, believing that the Elizabethan Settlement did not go far enough in reforming the medieval church, organized their own separatist congregations. Though many Puritans were harassed or forced to leave the country, a large Puritan or Presbyterian element remained in the Church of England.

When Elizabeth died in 1603, all religious parties welcomed her successor, James I: the Catholics because of his mother, Mary Queen of Scots; the Presbyterian Puritans because of his Presbyterian education; and the Anglicans because they thought his hostility to Presbyterian rule and his favorite expression, "No bishop, no king," indicated his preference for the Anglican position. The latter were correct.

Early in his reign James summoned a conference to meet with him at Hampton Court to consider the complaints of the Puritans and to settle their disputes with the bishops. He took no action on the Puritan grievances and the conference was about to end in failure, when John Reynolds, the Puritan leader and president of Corpus Christi College,

Oxford, moved that a new translation of the Bible be made because the current ones were "corrupt and not answerable to the truth of the original." The king, having translated some of the psalms himself, was immediately interested. He appointed a panel of fifty-four distinguished scholars who worked for seven years and finally produced the Authorized or King James Version of 1611. This version was the crowning achievement of nearly a century of translating, editing, and perfecting. Because of its superb quality, it became the undisputed English Bible and the Book that made the English a Bible-reading people.

Chapter 33 The Roman Catholic Revival

Even before the Protestant Reformation began, many people within the Catholic Church were calling for reform. A generation before Erasmus, Isabella, queen of Castile and joint sovereign of united Spain with her husband, Ferdinand, worked to make changes in the church. A sincerely pious woman of intellect and strong religious convictions, she appointed men of virtue and devotion to high offices in the Spanish church. Such was her religious zeal, however, that she tried to suppress heresy and banish the Jews from Spain. She was the mother of Catherine, the first wife of Henry VIII, and, as all the world knows, she offered to pawn her personal jewels in order to finance the voyage on which Columbus discovered the New World.

Aided by her confessor, Francisco Ximenes (Jimenez), Isabella attempted to correct abuses among the clergy and provide a better education for them. To that end Cardinal Ximenes established a university at Alcala. Here, during a fifteen year period, he supervised and financed an epoch-making undertaking—the compilation and printing of the many volumes of the Complutensian (Alcala) Polyglot Bible. This was a Bible for the learned rather than for ordinary people, because it was not in the vernacular but in Hebrew and Greek. The texts were printed side by side with Greek and Latin versions of those texts and other scholarly material. The Greek New Testament of the Polyglot Bible printed in 1514 was actually the first printed Greek text, but because it did not appear until the entire Bible was published in 1522, Erasmus was first in the field with his Greek text of 1516.

With the election of Paul III to the papacy in 1534, efforts to counter the devastating effects of the Protestant Reformation upon the Roman Catholic Church began in earnest. The new pope wrote a letter to Erasmus asking for his help in the unhappy quarrels rending the church, but Erasmus was then too old and ill for new undertakings. One of the pope's first actions was to reverse the policy for appointments to high office by choosing men outstanding for their religious ardor and learning rather than for their family position or wealth. He thereby provided the church with a series of wise and upright popes who infused it with a new spirit of devotion.

Next, he convened the Council of Trent and empowered it to make reforms and deal with disputed questions of belief. In its three sessions between 1546 and 1563, the Council rejected Protestant beliefs, confirmed the main points of Catholic theology, recognized the supremacy of the pope, passed statutes aimed at disciplining the lives of the clergy, and issued a uniform catechism and a standard edition of the Latin Bible, the Vulgate.

Because of the pope's great interest in art, he commissioned Michelangelo to paint the *Last Judgment* above the altar of the Sistine Chapel. When it was unveiled in 1541, it was seen as a tremendous assertion of the power of the church and a warning of the fate of heretics. In 1546 Paul III appointed Michelangelo to oversee the rebuilding of St. Peter's in Rome—the greatest architectural undertaking in Christendom. Working for the glory of God, Michelangelo brought together the work of previous architects in a structure that became the focus of the Roman Catholic Church and a symbol of its strength and pre-eminence.

In response to the Reformation, a heightened spirit of devotion within the Roman Church expressed itself in the rise of new ascetic orders and the reform of old ones. Chief among the new orders was the Society of Jesus, or the

Jesuit Order. It was founded by a former Spanish soldier, Ignatius Loyola, who had decided that instead of serving an earthly king he would become a soldier of Christ and strive for the greater glory of God. Six of his fellow students at the University of Paris joined him. After Paul III sanctioned their Order in 1540, it attracted men of intelligence who served with fervor and became highly disciplined and completely obedient to the general of their Society living in Rome.

At a time of great conflict within the Roman Church the Jesuits succeeded in deepening its spiritual life and strengthening the papacy. The schools and colleges they established became famous because the Jesuits were outstanding scholars in science and the humanities and the best schoolmasters in Europe. Their evangelizing activities took them everywhere, even to the Far East, where their most brilliant missionary was Francis Xavier. In the New World they conducted missions among the Huron and Iroquois tribes of North America. A Jesuit missionary, Jacques Marquette, discovered the Mississippi River. In South America they worked among the aborigines of Brazil and Paraguay. Eventually the Jesuits became the largest single religious order in the Roman Catholic Church, which their labors had helped to revive and make a great spiritual force.

Part Seven

Modern Christendom

Chapter 34 Aftermath of the Reformation

The map of Christendom changed drastically after the Reformation. Though the old division between the Orthodox churches of the East and the Catholic Church of the West still persisted, new divisions had now appeared in the West. As we have seen, the unity enjoyed by the Catholic Church during the Middle Ages ended when the northern parts of Europe became Protestant and England adopted Anglicanism. Scotland, the Scandinavian countries, Finland, Estonia, Latvia, the north German states, the western cantons of Switzerland, and the Dutch Republic all withdrew their allegiance from the Roman Catholic Church to form Protestant churches. In the rest of Europe—Italy, Spain, Portugal, France, the southern Netherlands, southern Germany, Ireland, Poland, Bohemia, Hungary—the Roman Church survived. Considerable overlapping existed in such places as France and Ireland, and there were Roman Catholic minorities in Great Britain and elsewhere. Yet, on the whole, the religious map of western Europe of 1600 remained fairly stable down to the present time.

The Roman Catholic Church, as the preceding chapter indicates, emerged from the Reformation stronger and more zealous than ever to revitalize Christianity. With its most flagrant abuses removed, its theological position

Aftermath of the Reformation

clearly defined by the Council of Trent, and the deepest needs of its people better served by its new religious orders, it stood on the threshold of a new age.

In Protestant lands the Reformation brought spiritual awakening. Bible reading became wide-spread, piety flourished, and there was renewed concern for others and for the salvation of individual souls. But Protestantism was weakened by its divisions. Besides the Lutheran, Calvinistic, and Anglican systems, there were other smaller, independent movements that challenged the theology and practices of the larger Protestant bodies.

The Puritans, a radical group in England opposed to what they regarded as remnants of Roman Catholic superstitions still surviving in the Church of England, wanted to purge its worship and purify many of its practices and doctrines. They believed that in the Bible, not the church, was the basic authority for Christianity. Because they upheld the idea of the priesthood of all believers, they were opposed to such matters as priestly vestments, which seemed to them to set the clergy apart in a special spiritual category. They advocated an ardent yet stern piety, unadorned churches, a rigid code of personal morals, and a reformed society. The religious life of the Puritan vision was expressed by John Bunyan in *Pilgrim's Progress.*

In the 17th century those who opposed the national, or the dominant, church usually suffered persecution because religious liberty or even tolerance was rare. In Europe only the Netherlands accorded a fairly broad degree of religious liberty and toleration, and consequently it became a refuge for the persecuted, including a group of Separatist Puritans, the English Congregationalists, who, as the Pilgrim Fathers, finally settled in the New World in 1620.

Chapter 35 Christianity Comes to America

Christianity was first brought to the New World in the 16th century by the Spanish conquerors of Central and South America. Following the conquerors came great numbers of Franciscan, Dominican, and Jesuit missionaries who set up mission systems for the conversion of the native populations. In 1551 and 1553 these missionaries founded the two oldest institutions of higher learning in the New World: the University of San Marcos in Lima, Peru, and the University of Mexico.

In 1604 the first settlement in Canada was made by Pierre de Monts, a Huguenot. Later, French Catholic colonists arrived, and under Francis de Laval, the first bishop of Quebec (1674-1688), the Roman Catholic Church became a vital force in the colony. Bishop de Laval is the main character in Willa Cather's novel of this period, *Shadows on the Rock.*

The rest of colonial America became the chief refuge for those who were persecuted in Europe for their religious convictions. Many came, of course, for political, economic, or social reasons, but almost every religious group that sprang from the Reformation sent some of its people to the New World. The four principal religious bodies of the colonial period were, in the order of their formation: Anglican, Congregational, Presbyterian, Baptist.

After Virginia was permanently founded at Jamestown in 1607, the Church of England was established by law as the official church, under the jurisdiction of the bishop of London. In due course the Church of England was named the official church in Maryland, North and South Carolina, New York, and Georgia, but in some of these colonies it was at a disadvantage because of the greater number of dissenting churches. In Virginia the bishop of London's representative, James Blair, a clergyman and missionary, founded the College of William and Mary at Williamsburg in 1693, the second oldest college in North America. With Harvard, established in 1636 by the Congregationalists, it heads the long, distinguished roster of colleges organized by churches. Among these was King's College, now Columbia University, founded in New York by royal grant in 1754 under its first president, Samuel Johnson, the clergyman who had held classes in the schoolhouse of Trinity Church.

When the colonial period came to an end and the independence of the United States was recognized in 1783, the Anglican churches, which had been under the care of the Bishop of London, began to organize themselves in the new circumstances. The Anglicans now called themselves Episcopalians and their churches Episcopal churches in order to show their loyalty to the ancient ministry of bishops in apostolic succession. At this point, however, there were no American bishops. In 1783, after the bishop-elect of Connecticut, Samuel Seabury, failed to obtain consecration in England because of a law requiring bishops to take the oath of allegiance to the crown, he went to Scotland. There the Scottish bishops were free to consecrate him without the oath, and on November 14, 1784, three bishops of the Scottish Episcopal Church consecrated Samuel Seabury as the first bishop of the Episcopal Church. This was the initial step in the extension of the Anglican episcopate overseas and around the world.

Two years later Parliament passed a law freeing bishops who were to be consecrated for churches outside the British dominions from the oath of allegiance to the crown. The archbishop of Canterbury then consecrated bishops-elect William White of Pennsylvania and Samuel Provoost of New York in 1787. The ceremony took place in the beautiful old chapel of Lambeth Palace where Matthew Parker had been consecrated more than two hundred years earlier and Wycliffe had been tried for heresy in the 14th century.

The first official American Prayer Book, revised and adapted to American needs, was issued by the General Convention of the church meeting in Philadelphia in 1789. Thus the Protestant Episcopal Church in the United States of America was established with its *Book of Common Prayer*, its bishops, and a democratic episcopal government. Though from Maine to Georgia, Episcopal churches had been established everywhere, they were fewer in number than the churches of the Congregationalists, the Presbyterians, or the Baptists. Nevertheless, more Episcopalians signed the Declaration of Independence than the members of any other colonial church.

Beginning with the settlement of the Pilgrim Fathers at Plymouth in 1620, great numbers of English Puritans made the long sea voyage across the Atlantic to escape persecution at home and to establish in the New World communities that would embody their Christian ideals. The Congregational colonies of Plymouth, Massachusetts Bay, Connecticut (Hartford), and New Haven formed theocratic Bible commonwealths under such leaders as John Winthrop and John Cotton in Boston, Richard Mather in Dorchester, Thomas Hooker in Hartford, and John Davenport in New Haven. According to the Congregational form of church government, each church was free to control its own affairs. Religious uniformity was required in each colony and dissidents were excluded from it. The Congregational book of discipline included the most notable expression of Calvinism, the Westminster Confession of 1647. With a grant from the Massachusetts Bay Colony and the bequest of

John Harvard, a graduate of Emmanuel College, Cambridge, Harvard College was founded in 1636 to train ministers for Congregational churches. John Harvard's bequest included 780 English pounds and his library of 320 volumes. By the end of the colonial period, though Congregational churches were largely confined to New England, they were more numerous than the churches of any of the other three principal religious bodies.

Roger Williams is generally considered to be the father of American Baptists. When he was banished from the Massachusetts Bay Colony for opposing coercion in religious matters, he took refuge in Rhode Island. At Providence in 1639 he and others who were seeking religious freedom founded the first Baptist church in America. The Baptists upheld the principles of separation of church and state, the believer's baptism by immersion, conversion as a condition of membership, the independence of the congregation, and individual responsibility to God. During the revivals of the 18th century and the great westward migrations the Baptists grew rapidly in numbers because their democratic form of government and their unsalaried and untrained ministry gave flexibility in establishing churches for people living under frontier conditions.

The Scots-Irish missionary Francis Makemie is called the father of American Presbyterianism because it was largely through his efforts that the Philadelphia presbytery was formed in 1706. Between 1720 and 1740 more than a hundred thousand Irish Presbyterians of Scottish descent, discontented with the economic and religious conditions imposed on them by the English government, came to America. Having come late to the colonies, these devout Presbyterians pushed energetically westward into West Virginia, western North Carolina, Kentucky, Tennessee, and other southern states. In order to provide educated ministers for their fast-growing churches, the Presbyterians in 1746 established the College of New Jersey, now Princeton University. John Witherspoon, president of the college, was the only clergyman to sign the Declaration of Independence. By the beginning of the Revolutionary War the Presbyterians were outranked only by the Congregationalists in the number of their churches.

In addition to the four largest religious bodies already mentioned, a number of smaller but influential sects were scattered through the American colonies. The oldest of these was the Dutch Reformed Church, which was established at New Amsterdam, now New York City, in 1628. Jonas Michaelius came from Holland to be its first minister. This and the other Reformed Churches followed Calvinistic doctrines and Presbyterian forms of government. Many of the historic colonial churches of the Hudson Valley, Long Island, New York, and New Jersey were built for the Dutch Reformed Church. In 1766 its classis, or presbytery, founded Queens College, now Rutgers University, in New Jersey.

Members of the Society of Friends, or Quakers, first came from England to Massachusetts in 1656 as missionaries proclaiming the teachings of their founder, George Fox. This English mystic and religious genius believed in the "Inner Light" in every person and preached that true Christianity expresses itself in a transformed, consecrated life. He hated formalism, abhorred slavery, and declared that war is unlawful for a Christian. Owing largely to the behavior of Quakers who testified against the Puritan church-state in Massachusetts, four of them were hanged on Boston Common. George Fox traveled through the colonies from New England to North Carolina and by his powerful preaching strengthened the beliefs of his followers. Before he died in 1691, he had introduced better discipline and the sober qualities which have distinguished the Quakers ever since.

William Penn, an eminent Quaker, obtained from Charles II in 1681 an enormous grant of land for a colony in what is now Pennsylvania. Determined to find in America the freedom denied Quakers elsewhere, he insisted on the principle of religious liberty. This became a basic principle of the American political system. Penn founded Philadelphia and opened the colony largely to Quaker settlers. For one hundred English pounds a person could buy a five-thousand-acre estate and a city lot in Philadelphia. By 1775, though the greatest concentration of Quakers was in Pennsylvania, there were Quaker meetings from Maine to Georgia.

William Penn's policy of religious freedom attracted to Pennsylvania people with a variety of religious beliefs. Mennonites from Germany and Switzerland, an evangelical Protestant sect noted for their plain dress and simplicity of living, found refuge in Germantown in 1683. Other German groups included the German Baptists, or Dunkers, the German Reformed, and the Lutherans. By 1748, when Henry M. Muhlenberg organized the first permanent Lutheran synod, the Lutherans were the largest religious group in Pennsylvania.

The Moravian Church was a revival of the Bohemian Brethren founded in 1457 by the followers of the martyred John Huss. Under the leadership of Count von Zinzendorf the Moravian Church became outstanding in the 18th century not only for its vital spiritual life but also for its missionary zeal. In 1741 Zinzendorf gave the Moravian settlement in Pennsylvania the name Bethlehem—a town that was to become the American headquarters of his movement and later a steel manufacturing center.

Among these smaller colonial bodies, the Quakers had 295 congregations; the Dutch and German Reformed, together, 251; the Mennonites and Dunkers, perhaps 20 each; the Moravians, about eight.

Though the Roman Catholics in the colonial period had only about 50 congregations, largely in Maryland and Pennsylvania, their number vastly increased with the enormous influx of immigrants from Ireland and southern Europe in the 19th and 20th centuries. Today, with their approximately fifty million members, they are the largest religious group in the United States.

Despite the existence of many different colonial churches, with all their richness and variety of faith and practice, the majority of the American people remained indifferent to religion until the Great Awakening quickened their Christian life and brought them into the various churches. Beginning in 1726 in the Dutch Reformed churches of New Jersey, this revival, with its great emotional appeal, swept through all the colonies and lasted for more than half a century. It preached a strict morality and earnest piety, and it emphasized the transforming nature of a "conversion." Under the forceful and logical preaching and writing of the theologian Jonathan Edwards at Northampton, Massachusetts, in 1734, the Great Awakening spread through New England, bringing twenty-five thousand new members into the churches there.

Methodism arrived in America during the Great Awakening. The movement had begun in England with John Wesley who, while a student at Oxford, formed a small religious group that included his brother Charles, the hymn writer, and John Whitefield, the great open-air preacher. Laughed at by the other students, and called "Methodists" because of their regular devotions and religious study, the group persisted. John Wesley became, and remained, a priest of the Church of England. He carried his evangelistic efforts everywhere, preaching in fields, in factories, and in churches, and traveling through England, Scotland, and Ireland. His message that salvation is from Christ alone and his emphasis on conversion and holiness made thousands of converts. Before he died in 1791 at the age of eighty-eight, it could be said that he and his fellow workers had revolutionized the religious life of the lower and middle classes of England.

Largely through one of Wesley's friends, the great revivalist preacher George Whitefield, who made six evangelistic tours of the colonies between 1740 and 1770, Methodism was established in America.

In 1784 Thomas Coke, acting on his authority from John Wesley, organized the Methodist Episcopal Church in America. Coke and the famous circuit rider Francis Asbury became the first bishops. The zeal of circuit riders and the fervor of camp meetings caused Methodist societies to spring up rapidly. Furthermore, the Methodist emphasis on free grace and individual responsibility to God was suited to people living in a democratic society. Three branches of Methodism united in 1939 to form the Methodist Church, which in 1968 joined with the Evangelical United Brethren Church—itself the result of a merger—to form the United Methodist Church, one of the strongest and most influential in the United States and around the world.

Chapter 36 The Christian Community Today

Amid the changes of the 19th and 20th centuries Christianity struggled against the challenge of a materialistic interpretation of life, yet it grew rapidly. It launched great missionary movements that proclaimed the message of Christ in every part of the world. It founded vital new churches, translated the Bible into more than sixteen hundred different languages and dialects, restudied its basic beliefs, gained fresh insights into the Scriptures, enriched its worship, tried to correct its errors, and pioneered in many kinds of humanitarian services. These innumerable and diverse achievements of the Christian community were brought about through the unstinting self-dedication and self-sacrifice of countless Christians. The story of Christianity's "advance through storm" during these years, a story of many people in many lands, would fill numerous volumes.

The religious liberty encouraged by Protestantism, while fostering development, also tended to produce many independent new churches. For instance, Congregationalists who did not believe in the doctrine of the Trinity came together in a new denomination to which, about 1815, the name Unitarian was given. One of their leaders was Ralph Waldo Emerson. Early in the 19th century Thomas and Alexander Campbell and others preached a primitive, simple gospel to which they hoped all Christians would rally, thus ending the scandal of sectarianism. But their followers finally broke away from the older churches to found the Disciples of Christ, now called the Christian Church.

Among other Christian bodies should be mentioned: the Mormons, founded by Joseph Smith in 1830; the Christian Scientists, founded by Mary Baker Eddy in 1879; the Assemblies of God, a pentecostal and missionary denomination founded in 1914; Jehovah's Witnesses, founded in 1931; and many others large and small that have influenced life in America.

The multiplicity of competing church bodies caused dismay among many Christians and their leaders. Inspired by their vision of the church, which Jesus described as "one flock [with] one shepherd" (John 10.16), the leaders began to move from fragmentation toward co-operation and unity. In the United States a beginning was made in 1905 when thirty churches agreed to form an agency for joint action. By the middle of the 20th century this became the National Council of the Churches of Christ in the United States of America, comprising some thirty-three Protestant and Eastern Orthodox denominations with a total membership exceeding forty million. In France, Switzerland, Britain, and Canada similar organizations were formed.

As the unification movement continued, it healed schisms caused by doctrinal differences within denominations and brought about numerous unions between separated churches. Around the world between 1925 and 1965 some thirty-seven mergers were made involving about one hundred and twenty-four church bodies.

On the world stage the ecumenical movement came of age when representatives from one hundred and fifty Protestant, Anglican, and Orthodox church bodies in some forty-four countries met in Amsterdam in 1948 to formally constitute the World Council of Churches. Thirty years later its membership had increased to more than two hundred.

The Roman Catholic Church entered into ecumenical relations with other churches as a result of the Decree on

Ecumenism passed by Vatican Council II (1962-1965). This decree encouraged co-operation by Catholics with "separated Churches and Communities" outside the Roman Church. During the short but significant pontificate of John XXIII (1958-1963) an opening was made toward the long-separated Orthodox churches of the East. Pope John, with the story of Joseph and his estranged brothers in mind, greeted the visiting head of the Greek Orthodox Church in five pregnant words, saying simply, "I am John, your brother."

Throughout the twenty centuries of its history, the church, as we have seen, has moved through storms and sunshine. This holy community of Christ's people in every age has been strengthened by the faith and spiritual depth of its individual members who, despite failures, occasional blindness, and all the weaknesses of human nature, continue to press forward. As Cyril F. Garbett, a recent archbishop of York, wrote, "The Church is an army on the march in hostile country, and not a rest camp for the tired."

On every front the church is challenged by materialistic standards and rapidly changing values. Christian truths are everywhere questioned, making the ministry of the church to the spiritual needs of humankind more difficult. Yet Christianity's message remains a living force, for now, as always, it permeates our civilization and prevails. Each new generation, struggling with the miseries of life and dissatisfied with mere existence, hungers for dignity, freedom, peace, and joy. People continue to ask, "Why am I living? What is the meaning of my life?" As was truly said long ago, "man does not live by bread alone" (Deuteronomy 8.3; Matthew 4.4). Today the world-wide community of Christ's people, the community of love, proclaims the good news that has always liberated men and women from bondage and brought them into newness of life. The promise endures: "And I, when I am lifted up from the earth, will draw all men to myself" (John 12.32).

Selected Bibliography

Baker, Archibald G., ed., *A Short History of Christianity*. Chicago: The University of Chicago Press, Phoenix Books, 1962. A comprehensive view in nontechnical language.

Booty, John E., *The Church in History*. New York: The Seabury Press, The Church's Teaching Series, 1979. Explains the great insights of the Christian tradition.

The Cambridge History of the Bible, 3 vols. Cambridge: The University Press, 1963-1970. An encyclopedic reference, giving the use, translations, study, and influence of the Bible from the beginning.

Cross, F. L. ed., *The Oxford Dictionary of the Christian Church*, 2nd ed. London: Oxford University Press, 1974. An indispensable reference book.

Dawley, Powel Mills, *Our Christian Heritage*, rev. ed. Wilton, Conn.: Morehouse-Barlow Co., 1978. The unique heritage of the Episcopal Church in the perspective of the long life of the Christian Church.

Latourette, Kenneth Scott, *Christianity Through the Ages*. New York: Harper and Row, Chapel Books, 1965. A brief account emphasizing the spread of Christianity.

Walker, Williston, *A History of the Christian Church*, 3rd rev. ed. by Robert T. Handy. New York: Charles Scribner's Sons, 1970. A revision of a 557-page standard text, long noted for its clarity and balance. Contains an extensive bibliography.

Index

Abelard, 91
Act of Supremacy, of 1534, 125; of 1559, 133
Acts of the Apostles, 2, 20
Aelia Capitolina, 16
Against Heresies, 22
Aidan, 70
Alaric, king of Visigoths, 58, 65
Alban, 29
Albertus Magnus, 76
Alcuin of York, 90
Alexandria, catechetical school in, 33, 34
Alfred, king of the West Saxons, 90-91
Ambrose, bishop of Milan, 56-57
Anastasis, 51
Anglican Communion, 136
Anglican episcopate, 146
Anselm, archbishop of Canterbury, 75, 91
Anthony Abbot, 60-61
Apocryphal gospels, 24
Apology, by Justin, 23
Apostles, 2, 5, 7, 10-11
Apostles' Creed, 22, 44
Apostolic Fathers, 30
Aquinas, Thomas, 76
Aramaic, 9, 14
Arian vs. Roman communion, 64
Arianism, 42, 44-46, 64
Aristotle, 76-77
Arius, 44, 45
Arles, Council of, 39
Armenia, 62
Asbury, Francis, 151
Assemblies of God, 153
Athanasius, patriarch of Alexandria, 25, 44, 46, 60, 100
Attila, king of Huns, 65

Augsburg Confession, 118
Augustine, bishop of Hippo, 10, 18, 48-49, 57-59; his *Confessions*, 58; his *City of God*, 58-59, 81
Augustine of Canterbury, 79

Bacon, Roger, 76-77
Baldwin I, king of Jerusalem, 86
Baptismal ceremonies, 53
Baptists, 147
Bar Kosiba, Simon, 15
Basil, bishop of Caesarea, 61
Basilica of the Savior, 50
Bath Abbey, 123
Beaufort, Lady Margaret, 108, 112, 124
Beloved Disciple, 2
Benedictine Order, 69, 71, 78
Bernard of Clairvaux, 72-73, 86
Bevan, Edwyn, 37
Bible, as basis of *Book of Common Prayer*, 133-34; and the humanists, 107, 110; in Middle Ages, 89-95; preservation of, 89-90; and the Reformation, 113, 127-29; reinterpreted by Christ, 4-5; study of, 33, 35, 49, 55, 73, 75-76, 89, 90, 91; use of, in art, 92-93; use of, in church, 23, 53-54, 55, 91; see also Gospels, New Testament, Translations of the Bible
"Bibles of the Poor," 91, 94
Bishops' Bible (English), 135
Blair, James, 145
Boleyn, Anne, 124, 125
Bonaventura, 76
Boniface, missionary to Germany, 71
Book of Common Prayer, 1559, 133; first official American, 146

INDEX

Book of Durrow, 70
Book of Kells, 70
von Bora, Katherine, 118
Bridget of Sweden, 84
Bulgarian Church, 101
Bunyan, John, 143
Byzantine Empire, 66, 85
Byzantine rite, 103
Byzantium, 41; *see also* Constantinople

Calvin, John, 119-21
Calvinism, 121
Campbell, Alexander, 152
Canterbury Cathedral, 27, 93
Cassiodorus, 68-69
Catherine of Aragon, queen, 123, 139
Catherine of Siena, 84
Caxton, William, 108
Celtic Christianity, 63-64
Celtic monasticism, 69-71
Chalcedon, Council of, 45-46, 96
Charlemagne, 59, 80, 81, 90
Charles V, 112, 124
Chaucer, 88
Christendom's divisions, 143
Christian faith, its appeal, 18; dawn of, 2; defended by Origen, 35; as expressed in Paul's letters, 13; formulated in creeds, 22, 45-46; and reason, 75; scriptural basis of, 24, 77
Christian Scientists, 153
Chrysostom, John, patriarch of Constantinople, 55-56
Church, as "catholic," 27; early years of, 7-8; in Middle Ages, 67, 105-6; in Renaissance, 106; Tertullian's description of, 38; in today's world, 152-54; unity of, lost, 142
Church music, 56-57, 79-80, 118
Church of England, 124-25, 129, 136, 137; in colonial America, 144-46
Churches built by Constantine, 41, 50-51

Church of St. John Lateran, Rome, 50
Church of the Holy Sepulcher, Jerusalem, 51-52, 85
Church worship, 53-55
Cistercian Order, 72-73
1 and 2 Clement, 30
Clement of Alexandria, 33
Clotilda, 64
Clovis, king of the Franks, 64
Cluniac Order, 72
Codex, 20-21
Codex Argenteus, 63
Codex Sinaiticus, 30, 41-42
Codex Vaticanus, 41-42
Coke, Thomas, 151
Colet, John, 110, 122-23
Colossians, 21
Columba, 70
Columbia University (King's College), 145
Complutensian Polyglot Bible, 139
Congregationalists, 145, 152; colonies of, 146-47; churches of, 146-47
Constance, Council of, 84
Constantine, 39-42, 45
Constantinople, 41, 55, 96, 98, 103, 106
Constantinople, Council of, 45-46
Coptic Church, 100
Cornelius, 10
Cotton, John, 146
Coverdale, Miles, 128, 131, 135
Cranmer, Thomas, archbishop of Canterbury, 125, 127, 130-31, 132
Cromwell, Thomas, 126-27, 128-29
Crusades, 85-87
Cybele, Great Mother, 17
Cyprian, 34
Cyril, 101
Cyrillic, 101
Cyril, patriarch of Alexandria, 99

Dante, 76
Davenport, John, 146
Dead Sea Scrolls, 36

Decius, emperor, 28
Diaspora, 12
Diatessaron, 24
Didache, 31
Diocletian, emperor, 28
Disciples of Christ, 152
Dodd, Charles H., 4
Dominican Order, 73-74, 76
Domitian, emperor, 26
Donne, John, 134
Dunkers, 149
Duns Scotus, 77
Dutch Reformed Church, 148, 149, 150

Eastern Orthodox Church, 97, 101-4, 154
Ecumenical Patriarch of Constantinople, 103
Eddy, Mary Baker, 153
Edict of Toleration, 39
Edward VI, king of England, 126, 130-31
Edwards, Jonathan, 150
Ein' Feste Burg, 118
Elizabethan Settlement, 135-36, 137
Elizabeth I, queen of England, 125, 133-37
Emerson, Ralph Waldo, 152
Ephesus, Council of, 99
Episcopalians, 145
Epistle of Barnabas, 30
Epistle to Diognetus, 32
Epistles of Ignatius, 31
Erasmus, Desiderius, 109-14, 117-18, 122-23, 125, 128, 139, 140
Etheria (Egeria), 52
Ethiopian Church, 100
Eucharist, 54
Eudoxia, empress, 56
Eusebius, 15, 16, 36, 39, 41, 45, 51

Faith, *see* Christian faith
Fathers of the Church, 30-36, 112
Finnian, 69
First Prayer Book of Edward VI, 131

Fisher, Bishop John, 112, 113, 125
Flavia Domitilla, 26
Flavian, Bishop Alexander, 16
Flavius Clemens, 26
Forty-two Articles, 131, 134
Fourth Lateran Council, 83
Fox, George, 148
Fragments from Papias, 31-32
Franciscan Order, 73-74, 76, 77
Francis of Assisi, 73-74
Friars, 73-74
Froben, John, 112
Frumentius, 100
Fulda, 71

Galerius, emperor, 39
Gamaliel, 7
Garbett, Cyril F., archbishop of York, 154
Geneva, 120-21
Geneva Bible (English), 121, 135
Gentiles, 10, 11
German Reformed, 149
Glosses, vernacular, 91
Gnostic documents, 21-22
Gnosticism, 21-22, 23
Godfrey of Bouillon, 86
Gospels, 2, 13-14; early pre-eminence of, 20, 24; Gospel books, 91-92; sources of, 7; theme of, 4-5; *see also* Bible, New Testament
Gothic architecture, 93-94
Great Awakening, 150
Great Bible (English), 121, 128-29, 135
Gregorian chant, 79-80
Gregory, bishop of Tours, 67
Gregory of Nyssa, 61
Gregory I, pope, 78-80, 89
Gregory VII, pope (Hildebrand), 78, 81-82
Gregory, the Illuminator, 62
Gutenberg Bible, 108

Hagia Sophia, 52-53, 87, 98
Harvard College, 145, 147

INDEX

Harvard, John, 146-47
Hebrews, 20
Helena, 41
Henry IV, German emperor, 82
Henry VIII, of England, 110, 112, 123-26, 129
Herbert, George, 134
Heresies, 20-22
Herod Agrippa I, 10
Hexapla, 35-36
Holy Spirit, 6, 10
Hooker, Richard, 136
Hooker, Thomas, 146
Hugh of St. Victor, 91
Huguenots, 121, 144
Humanists, Humanism, 106-7, 109-10, 112, 119, 122-23
Huss, John, 95

Iconoclastic Controversy, 97
Iconoclasts, destruction by, 126-27
Ignatius, bishop of Antioch, 27, 31
"Indulgences," 116
Innocent I, pope, 56
Innocent III, pope, 82-83
Institutes of the Christian Religion, 120
Iona, 70
Irenaeus, bishop of Lyons, 22, 33, 53
Irish monastic schools, 69-70
Isabella, queen of Castile, 139
Isis, 17
Islam, 101

James, apostle, 10
James I, king of England, 137-38
James, Letter of, 20
James, the Lord's brother, 11, 15
Jehovah's Witnesses, 153
Jerome, 16, 46, 48, 58, 61
Jerome of Prague, 95
Jerusalem, 1, 6, 10, 15, 16, 51-52; council of, 11; kingdom of, 86; patriarchate of, 96, 103
Jesuit Order, 141

Jesus Christ, beliefs concerning person and nature of, 4, 21-22, 24, 44-46, 99, 100; entombment of 1; resurrection of, 2, 4-6; witnesses to, 5
Jewel, John, 136
Jewish Christianity, 15-16
Jewish Christians, Greek-speaking, 9
Jews vs. Gentiles, 10-12
Joel, 6
John, apostle, 2, 4, 7, 11
John, Gospel of, 14
I John, Letter of, 21
John XXIII, pope, 154
Johnson, Samuel, president of Columbia College, 145
Judaism, 6, 7, 9, 15, 18
Jude, Letter of, 20
Julian, "the Apostate," 42
Justinian, emperor, 52, 98
Justin Martyr, 23, 28, 32-33

King James Version (English), 135, 138
King's College Chapel, Cambridge, 123
Knights Hospitalers, 86
Knights Templars, 86
Knox, John, 121
Kublai Khan, 100

Lambeth Palace, 135, 146
Langton, Stephen, archbishop of Canterbury, 83
Last Judgment, Michelangelo's, 140
Last Supper, 8
Latimer, Hugh, 128, 132
Latourette, Kenneth Scott, 62-63
de Laval, Francis, bishop of Quebec, 144
Lectionaries, 54
Leo I, pope, 65-66, 78, 96
Leo III, emperor, 97
Leo III, pope, 81
Leo X, pope, 112, 116, 123

Lindisfarne, 70; Gospels from, 70-71
Loch Ness monster, 70
Lollards, 51
London, parks of, 126
Lord's Supper, 54
Loyola, Ignatius, 141
Luke, 4; Gospel of, 14
Luther, Martin, 77, 114-18
Lutheran Church, 118
Lutherans, 149

Macarius, bishop of Jerusalem, 51
Macrina, 61
Magna Charta, 83, 122
Makemie, Francis, 147-48
Marcion, 23-24
Marcionites, 24
Marcus Aurelius, emperor, 28
Mark, Gospel of, 14
Marquette, Jacques, 141
Martel, Charles, 71, 80, 101
Mar Thoma Church, 11, 99
Martin of Tours, 61
Mary Magdalene, 2
Mary, queen of England, 124, 125, 131-32
Mary, queen of Scots, 110, 121, 137
Mather, Richard, 146
Matthew Bible (English), 128
Matthew, Gospel of, 14
Matthias, apostle, 5
Melanchthon, Philip, 118
Melito, bishop of Sardis, 16
Mennonites, 149
Mestrop, 62
Methodism, in America, 151; origins in England, 150
Methodius, 101
Mexico, University of, 144
Michelangelo, 140
Milan, Edict of, 40
Milvian bridge, battle at, 39-40
Missionary outreach, 5, 7, 9, 10, 17, 34, 38-39, 62-64, 70-71, 79, 99-101, 141, 144-51, 152

Mithras, 18
Monasteries, supression of, 126-27
Monasticism, beginnings of, 60-61; in Middle Ages, 68-74, 89-90
Monophysitism, 46, 100
de Monts, Pierre, 144
Moravian Church, 149
More, Sir Thomas, 110, 113, 122-23, 124, 125
Mormons, 153
Moslem conquests, 101
Muratorian Fragment, 25
Muhlenberg, Henry M. 149

National Council of Churches of Christ, 153
Nero, emperor, 13, 26
Nestorianism, 46, 99-100
Nestorius, 99
New Testament, authority of, 13, 33, 53, 77; canon of, 25, 42, 46; Greek text of, 112, 139; Paul and, 13; sayings and stories of Jesus in, 1, 13; textual study of, 35; writing of, 13-14; see also Bible, Gospels
Nicaea, Council of, 42, 45
Nicene Creed, 45, 61
Northumbria, 70

Olivetan, 119
Orders, religious, 69, 72-74, 140-41
Origen, 16, 28, 34-36

Pachomius, 61
Papacy, 78-84; at Avignon, 83-84
Papal powers, 105-6
Papias, bishop of Hierapolis, 5, 31-32
Parker, Matthew, archbishop of Canterbury, 134-35, 146
Patriarchates, 96, 103
Patrick, apostle to Ireland, 63, 69
Paula, 61
Paul, apostle, 4, 9, 11-12, 13, 17; letters of, 5, 13, 20, 21
Paul III, pope, 125
Pelagius, 57-58

INDEX

Pella, 15
Penn, William, 148-49
Pentecost, 4, 6
Pepin, king of the Franks, 80-81; Donation of, 81
Persecution of Christians, 7, 9, 13, 26-29, 34, 45
1 and 2 Peter, 20
Peter, apostle, 2, 4, 6, 7, 10, 11, 13, 78
Peter Lombard, 91
Peter the Hermit, 86
Philip II, king of Spain, 131
Pilgrimages, to Holy Land, 51-52, 85, 87; to Rome, Compostella, Canterbury, 87
Pilgrim Fathers, 143, 146
"Pilgrim of Bordeaux," 52
Pilgrim's Progress, 143
Pole, Cardinal Reginald, 131, 134
Polo, Marco, 100
Polycarp, bishop of Smyrna, 22, 27; *Epistle of,* 31; Martyrdom of, 31
Presbyterians, 121; derivation of name, 120; in colonial America, 147-48
Princeton University (College of New Jersey), 147-48
Protestant, origin of name, 118
Provoost, Samuel, bishop of New York, 146
Puritans, 121, 137, 143, 146

Quakers, 148, 149

Reformation, antecedents of, 105-8; Calvin and, 119-21; in England, 122-38; Erasmus and, 109-14; Luther and, 115-18; in Roman Catholic Church, 139-41
Resurrection, 2, 4
Reynolds, John, 137-38
Ridley, Nicholas, bishop of London, 132
Rogers, John, 128, 132
Roman Empire, accepts Christianity, 40-43; breakdown of, 58, 65-66; dominance of, 17; paganism in, 17-18; persecutes Christians, 26-29
Roman Catholic Church, 97, 139, 140, 153-54; in colonial times and today, 149-50
Russian Church, 101-102
Rutgers University (Queens College), 148

Sadducees, 7
St. Denis, near Paris, 93-94
St. Paul's, London, 130
St. Peter's, Rome, 50-51, 81, 116, 140
Sanhedrin, 7, 9
San Marcos, University of, 144
Saul, *see* Paul
Sayings of Jesus, 1
Schism, the Great, 96-97
Scholasticism, 75-77
Scotland, 70, 121
Scriptures, *see* Bible
Seabury, Samuel, bishop of Connecticut, 145
Septuagint, 23, 35, 46
Serbian Church, 101
Seven liberal arts, 90
Shakespeare, 121, 134
Shepherd of Hermas, 30, 31
Simeon, of Jewish-Christian Church, 15
Smith, Joseph, 153
Society of Jesus, *see* Jesuit Order
Somerset, duke of, 130
Stephen, martyr, 9
Stephen II, pope, 80
Suger, Abbot, 93
Summa Theologiae, 76
Syrian Monophysite Church, 100-101

Tatian, 24
Tertullian, Church Father, 10, 33-34, 38
Tewkesbury Abbey, 126

Theodoric the Great, emperor, 68
Theodosius the Great, emperor, 57
I Thessalonians, 13
Thirty-nine Articles, 134
Thomas, apostle, 2, 11
Tiridates, king of Armenia, 62
Translations of the Bible, 46, 48-49, 62-63, 91, 95, 101, 117, 119, 120, 121, 127-29, 138
Trent, Council of, 140
Tyndale, William, 127-28

Ulfilas, apostle to the Goths, 62, 63
Unitarians, 152
United Methodist Church, 151
Urban II, pope, 85

Valentinian III, emperor, 78
Vatican Council II, 154
Vatican Library, 107
Visigoths, 62
Vladimir, Grand Prince, 101
Vulgate, 48, 69, 90, 92, 95

Walker, Williston, 79

Wesley, John, 150
Westminster Abbey, 127, 130
Westminster Confession, 1647, 146
William and Mary, College of, 145
William the Conqueror, king of England, 82
William of Ockham, 77
William of Orange, 121
Williams, Roger, 147
Winthrop, John, 146
Witherspoon, John, 148
Whitefield, John, 150
White, William, bishop of Pennsylvania, 146
Women at tomb, 2
World Council of Churches, 103, 153
Worms, Edict of, 116-17
Wycliffe, John, 88, 94-95, 107, 135

Xavier, Francis, 141
Ximenes, Francisco, cardinal, 139

von Zinzendorf, Count, 149
Zwingli, Ulrich, 120